Carving the Green-Wing Teal

QuickTips for Hen and Drake

Jeffrey Moore

Schiffer Publishing Ltd

4880 Lower Valley Road, Atglen, PA 19310 USA

Text written with and photography by Donna S. Baker

Library of Congress Card Number: 00-110006

Designed by John P. Cheek
Type set in ZapfHumanist Dm BT/ZapfHumanist BT

ISBN: 0-7643-1314-2
Printed in China

Published by Schiffer Publishing Ltd.
4880 Lower Valley Road
Atglen, PA 19310
Phone: (610) 593-1777; Fax: (610) 593-2002
E-mail: Schifferbk@aol.com
Please visit our web site catalog at
www.schifferbooks.com
We are always looking for people to write books on new and related subjects. If you have an idea for a book, please contact us at the above address.

This book may be purchased from the publisher.
Include $3.95 for shipping.
Please try your bookstore first.
You may write for a free catalog.

In Europe, Schiffer books are distributed by
Bushwood Books
6 Marksbury Avenue
Kew Gardens
Surrey TW9 4JF England
Phone: 44 (0) 20 8392 8585
Fax: 44 (0) 20 8392 9876
E-mail: Bushwd@aol.com
Free postage in the UK. Europe: air mail at cost.

Contents

Introduction

The Green-Wing Teal

The green-wing teal is the smallest of North American waterfowl with an average weight of only twelve ounces. Known for its comical, non-stop motion and vocal imitation, the green-wing is one of the most colorful and easily distinguished of the dabbling ducks.

The spring migration of the green-wing is an early one. Breeding grounds can be found in Canada, Alaska, and other areas of the northern United States. Nesting on the ground, in thickets or tall grass, the hen may lay seven to fifteen eggs between May and August. The incubation period of the green-wing is twenty-one to twenty-three days and care of the nest rests entirely with the hen. Immature ducklings resemble the hen of the species.

Being a dabbler, green-wings feed in streams and marshes, primarily on grass and other vegetation. They will forage on the ground for acorns, seeds, berries, and also farm grains. Green-wing teals seen traveling in small flocks may resemble shore birds in their uniformed flight patterns. They are quick, agile fliers often seen traveling with larger dabbling ducks.

Spend some time getting acquainted with the green-wings in their natural habitat. It will be an invaluable lesson that will provide you with a true feel for this comical, animated little duck.

Tools

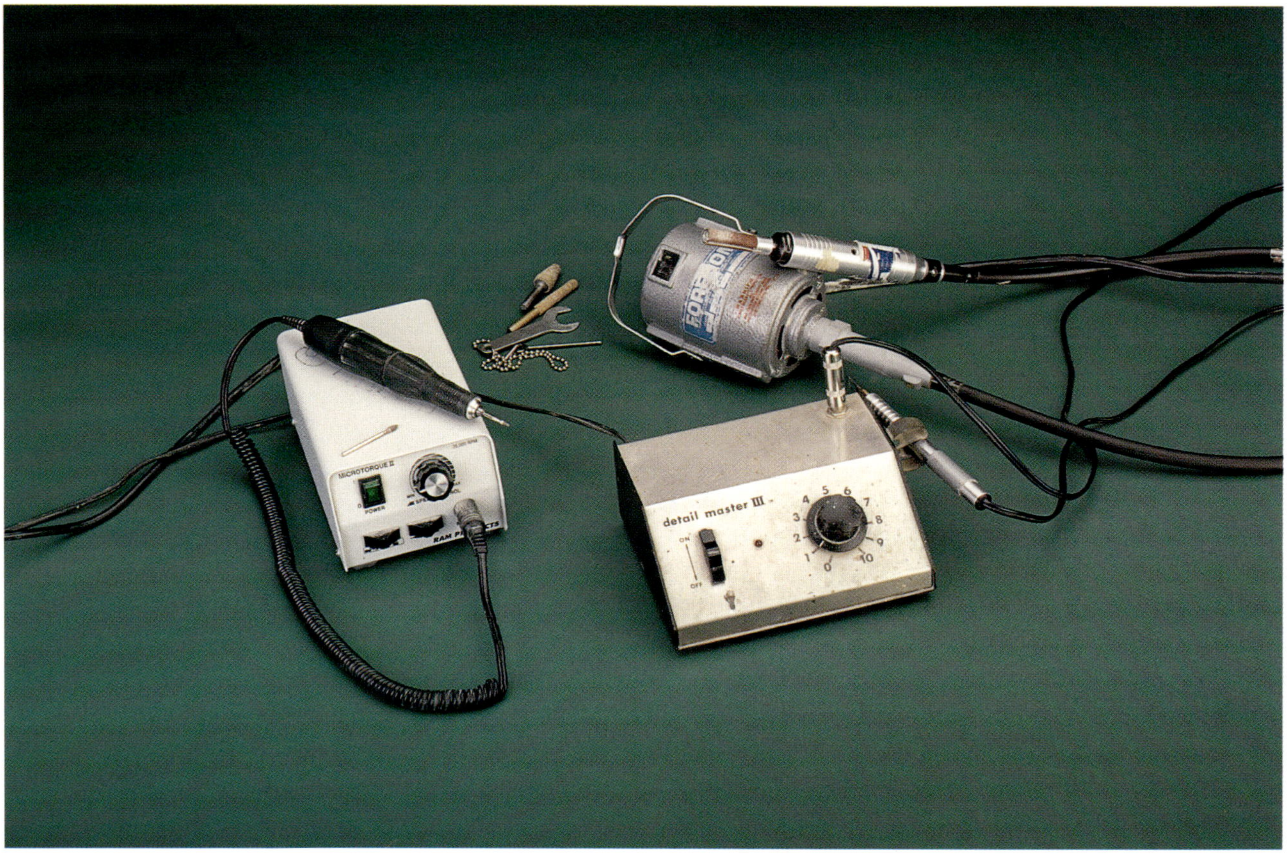

Here are the basic carving tools used in this book. Clockwise, from top right: Foredom tool, 22,000 RPM variable collet rotary tool used for general shaping and sanding (shown with assorted bits and key); Detail Master III, 50 watt variable temperature burning unit used for adding detail; Ram tool, 35,000 RPM high speed texturizing tool used with rubies, diamonds, and stones for adding very fine details.

Drake, top view.

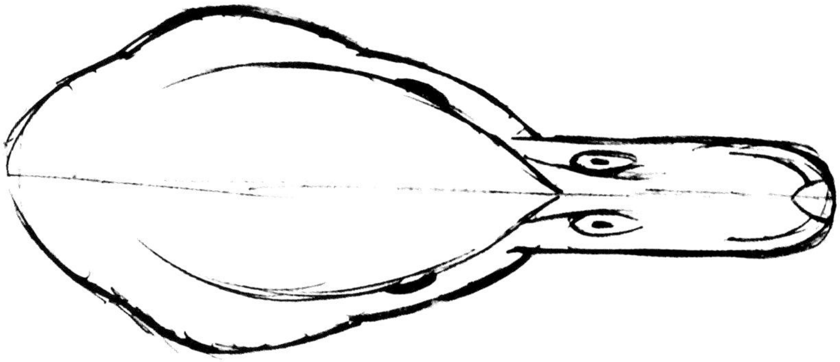

Hen head.

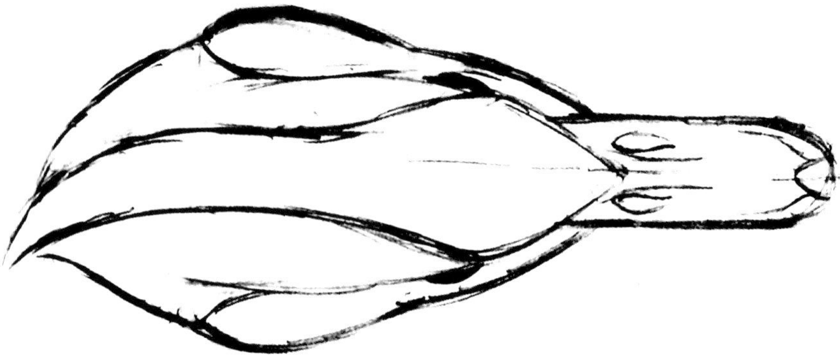

Drake head.

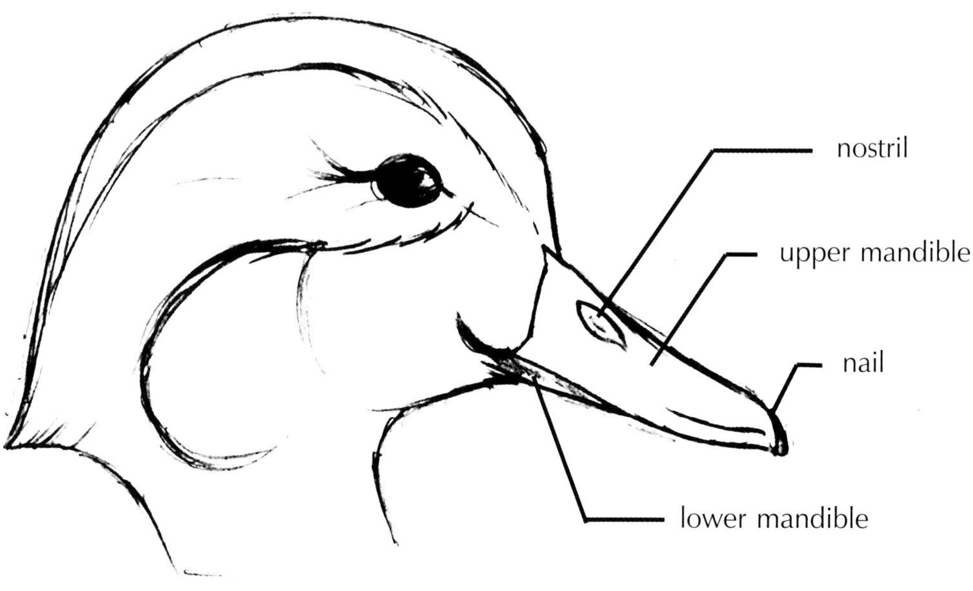

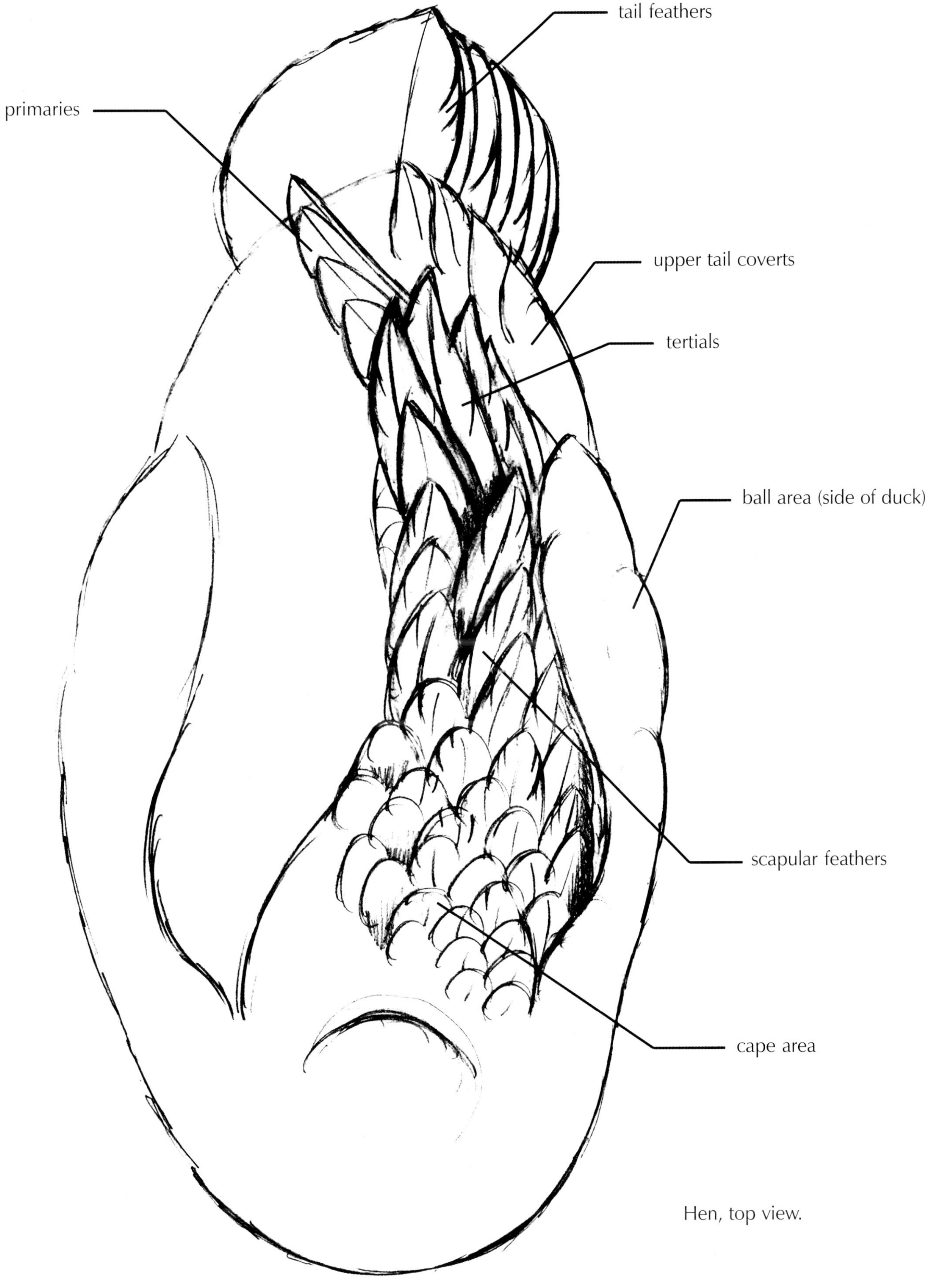
tail feathers
primaries
upper tail coverts
tertials
ball area (side of duck)
scapular feathers
cape area

Hen, top view.

Hen, head up.

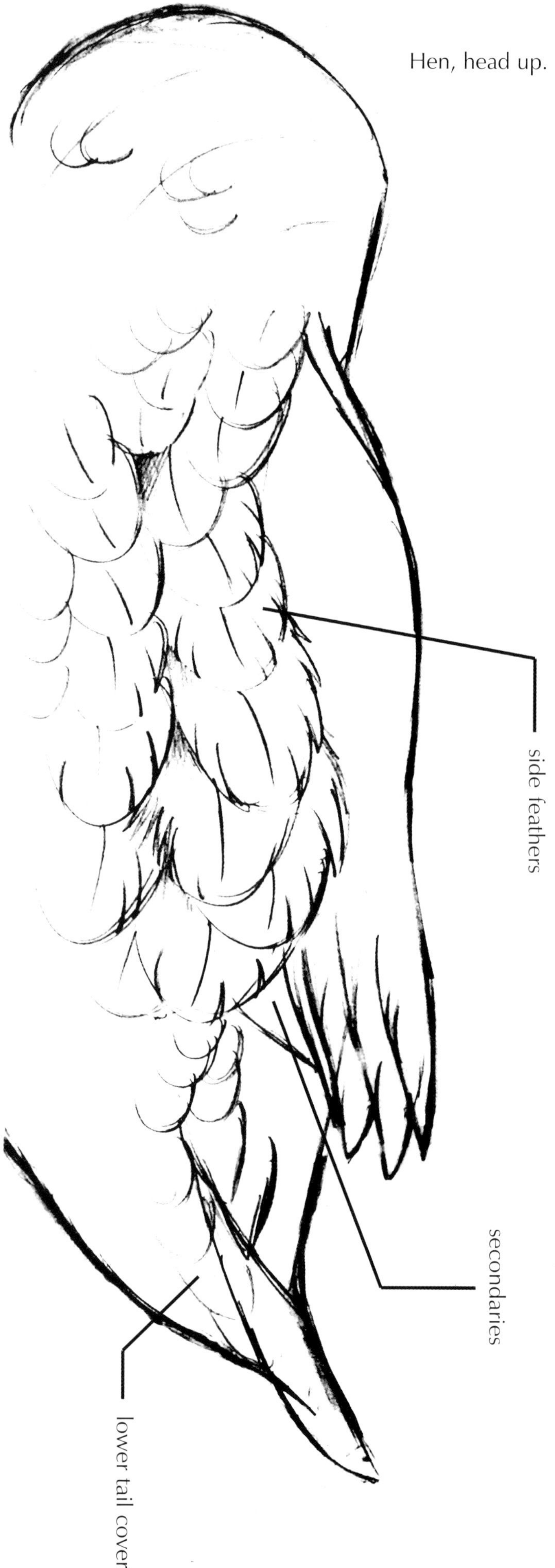

Hen, head down.

Color Chart

Gesso Colors

Gray Gesso

White Gesso + Raw Sienna

Brown Gesso

Blocking Colors

Burnt Sienna

Yellow Oxide

Thalo Green

Black

Airbrushed Colors

White

70% White +
15% Raw Sienna +
15% Burnt Sienna

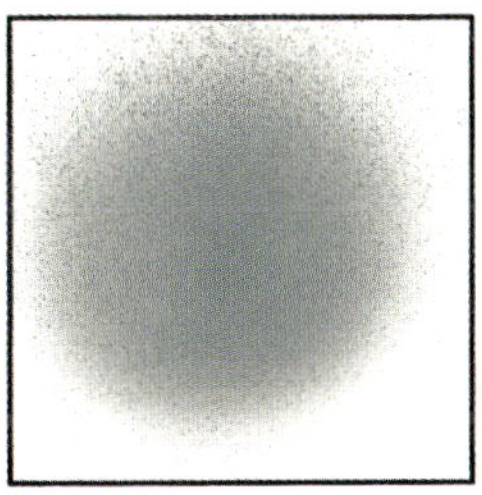

Gray

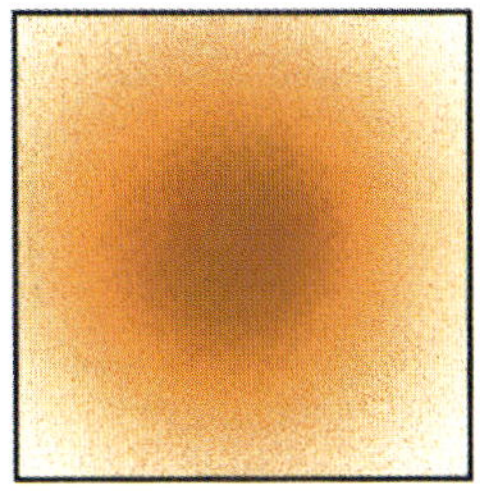

Raw Sienna

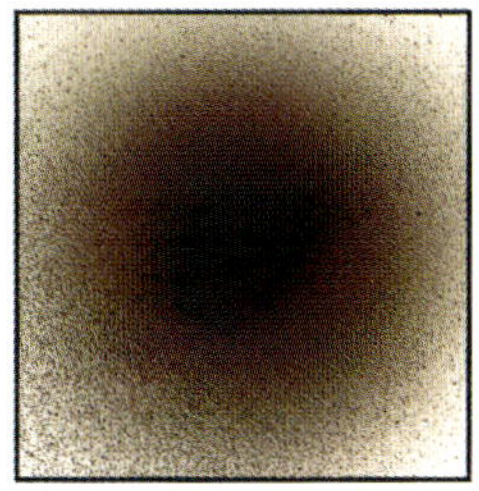

70% Burnt Umber +
30% Raw Sienna
(Hen Brown)

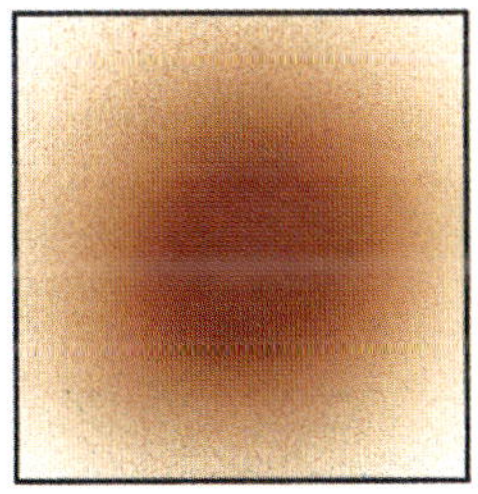

Burnt Sienna

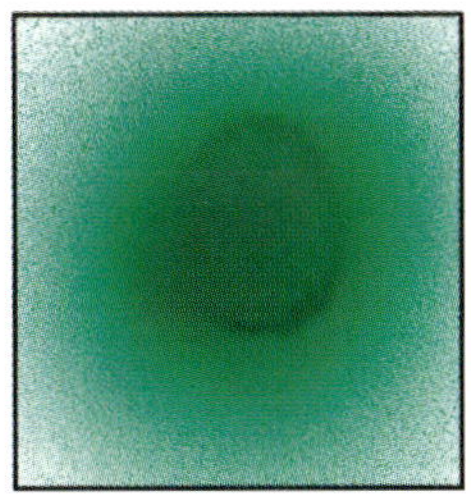

Iridescent Green

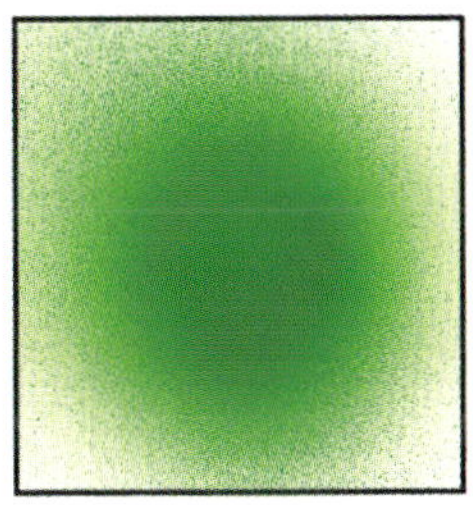

Iridescent Yellow/Green

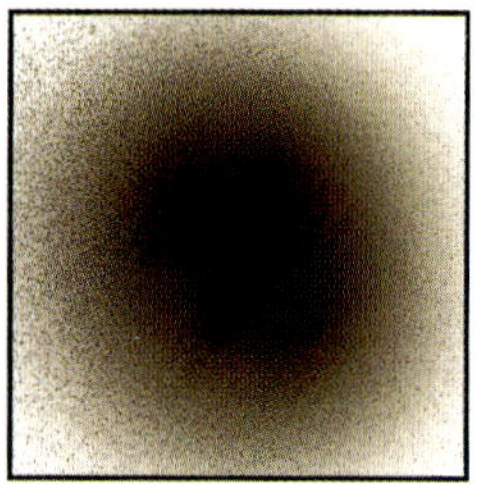

Burnt Umber

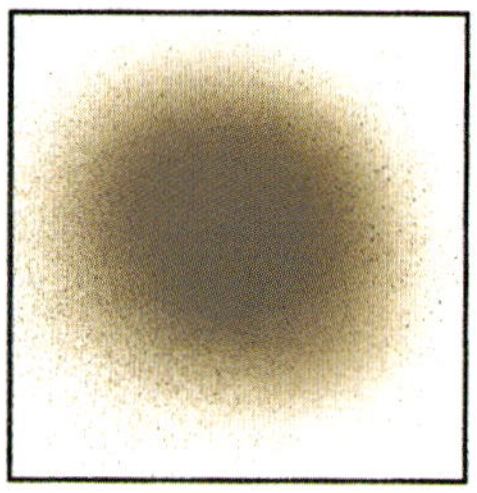

70% White +
15% Raw Sienna +
15% Burnt Umber (Tan)

80% White +
20% Raw Sienna

Detailing Colors

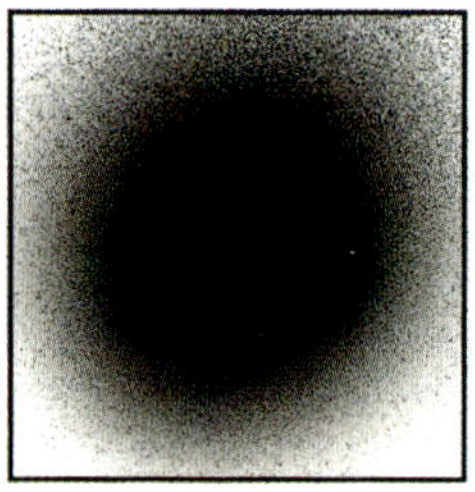

Black

Detail of Vermiculation

50% Yellow Oxide +
50% White

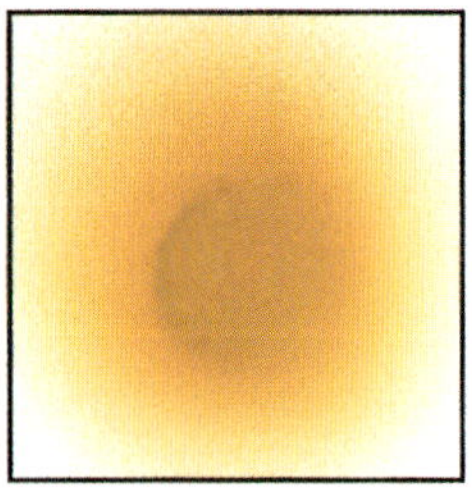

50% Yellow Oxide +
50% White

80% Raw Sienna +
20% White

80% White +
20% Yellow Oxide

Carving and Burning

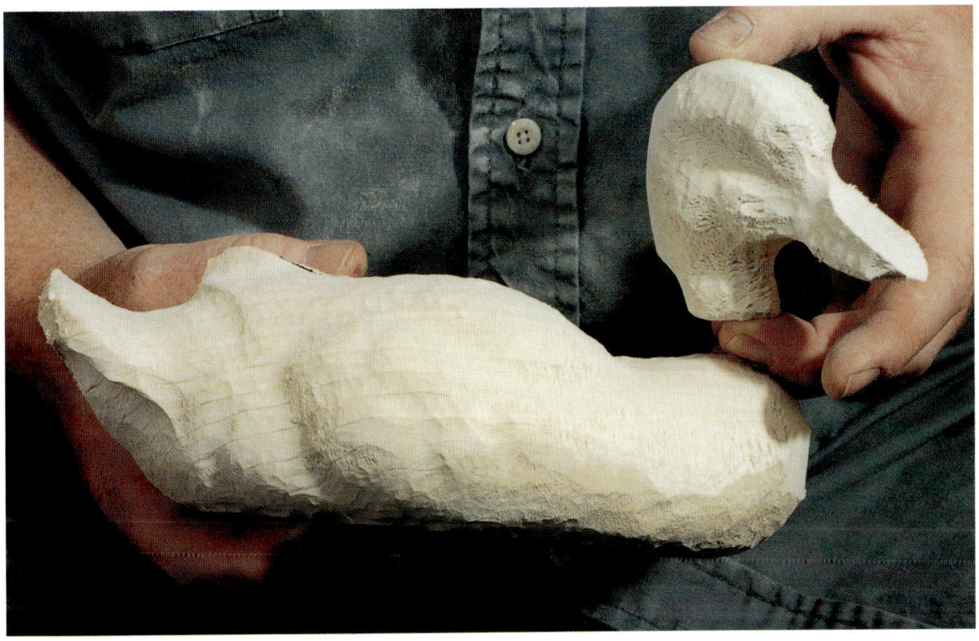

For both the hen and drake, we will start with a rough out — a preshaped, duplicated bird. These rough outs come from Fowl Play Studios, but the same techniques that follow can be applied to rough outs available from other sources. Here is the rough out for the body and head of the drake.

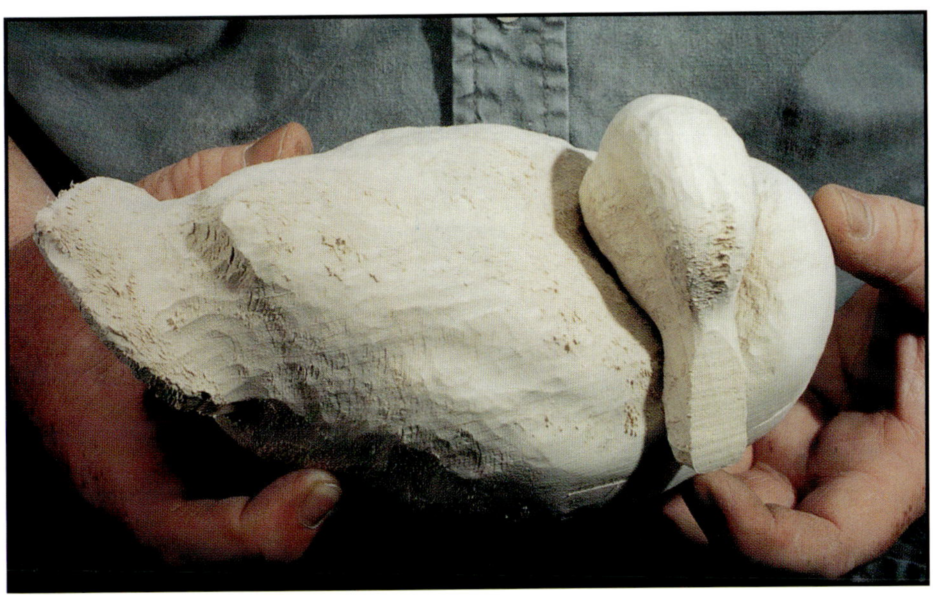

And here is the rough out for the hen.

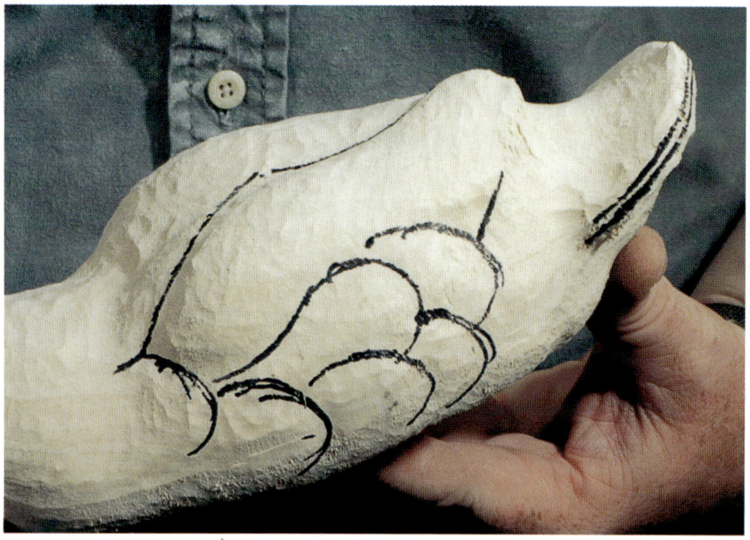

I have drawn lines on the body of the drake where we will be using the carbide tool. Although I normally use a pencil, I am using a marker here so you can see the lines more easily.

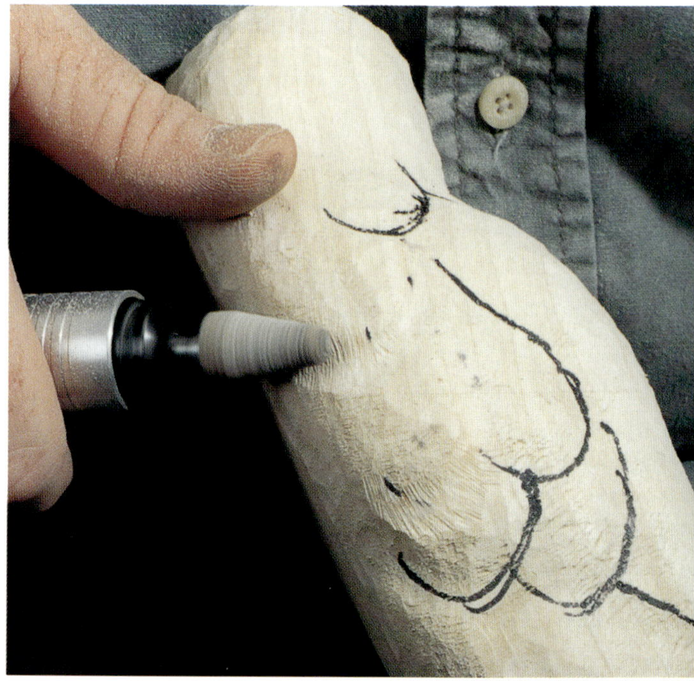

I am using the carbide tool to lightly define the feather groups. Bracing your hand with your thumb will give you greater control while using the tool. Complete this step on both sides.

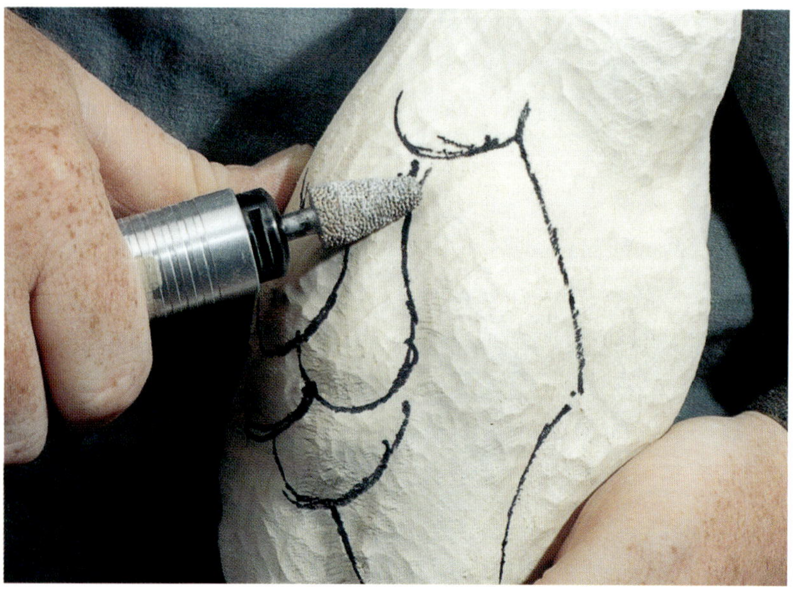

Using a 44b hand piece, start here with the rough carving.

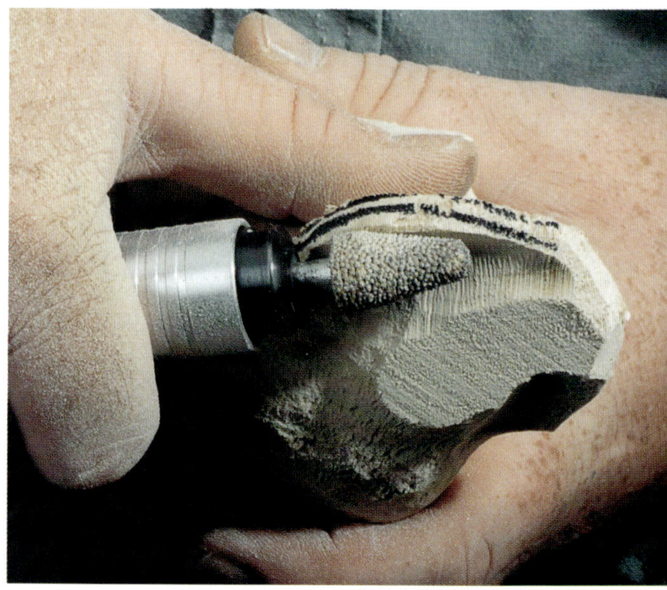

Thin down the tail with the carbide.

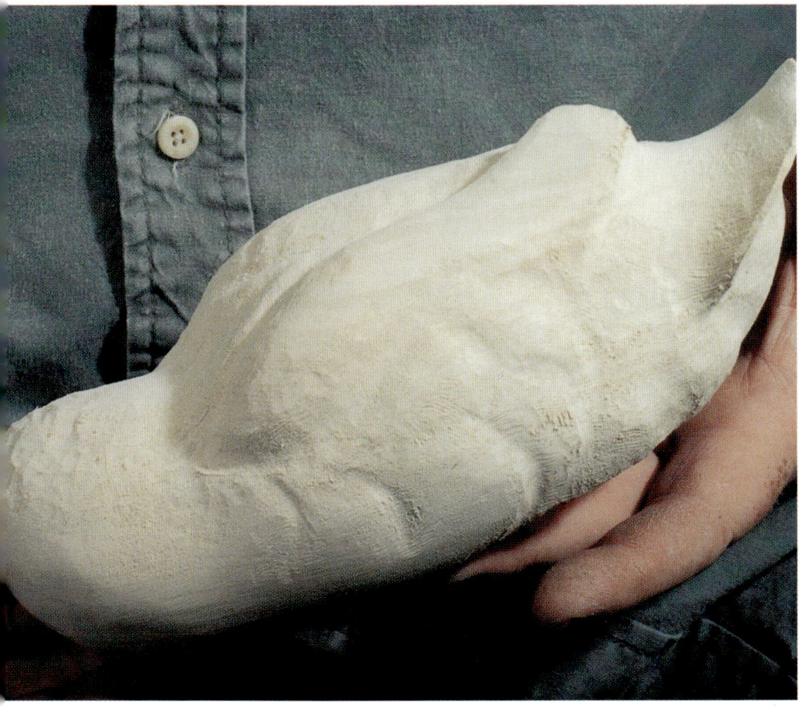

Here's what the feather groups should look like when you have finished with the carbide.

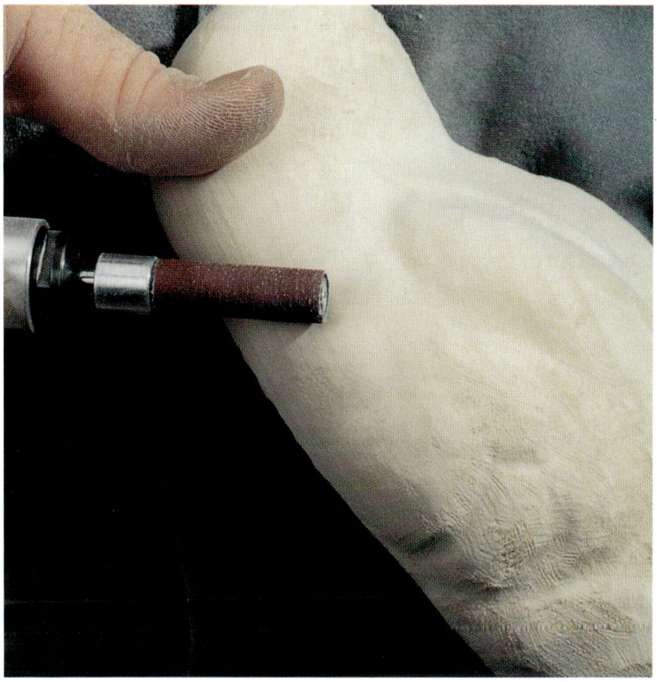

Next, sand the bird using a sponge sander. Go over the entire bird, paying special attention to the lines created by carbiding. You can see the difference here between a rough area and a sanded one.

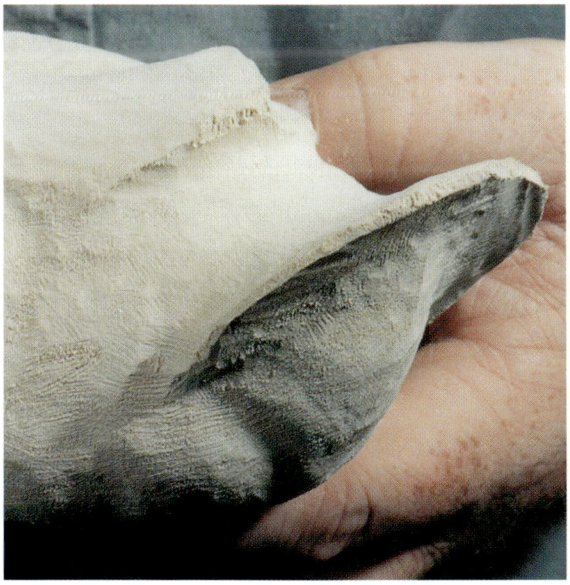

The completed carbided tail should look like this.

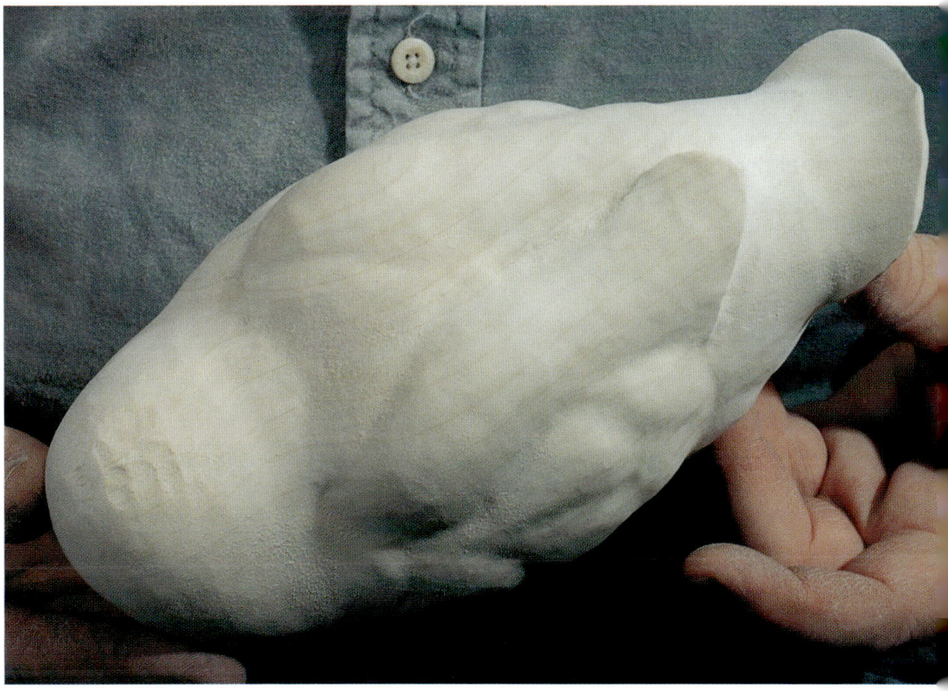

The completely sanded bird.

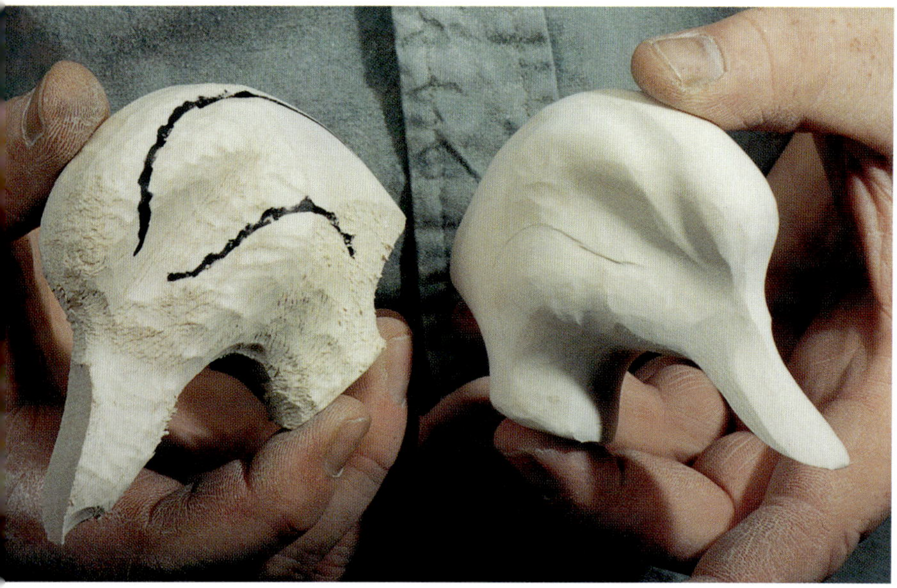

When you have completed the body, work on the head. On the left is a rough duplicated head with lines drawn to define the iridescent green patch that is characteristic of the green-wing teal drake. On the right is the head after it has been sanded all over with the sponge sander.

The same view for the hen head: a rough duplicated head on the left, a completely sanded head on the right.

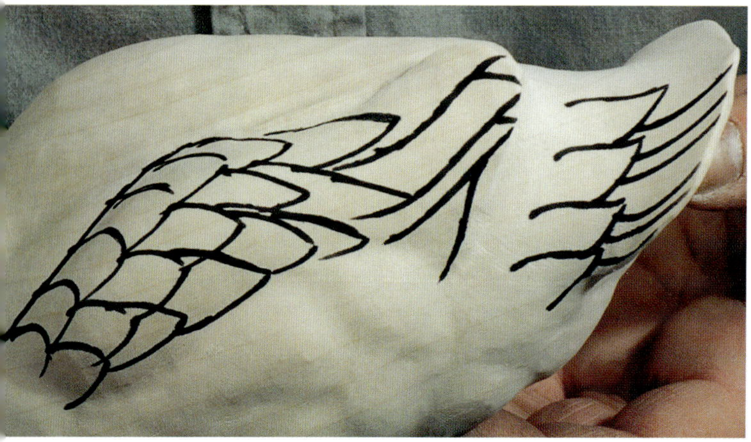

In preparation for using the high speed texturing tool (Ram tool), draw the individual feathers on the back and the tail.

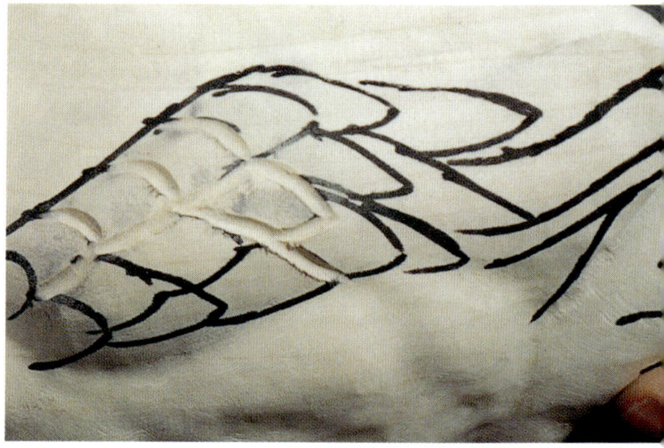

I will be using a number 19 ruby to outline all the feathers. Here I have outlined four of the scapular feathers.

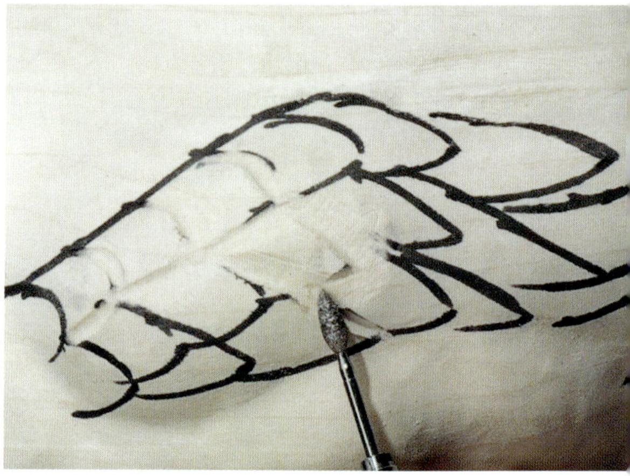

Next, use the ruby to sand down and soften the wood around each feather. I'm pointing to the area that I have just done.

Now soften the edge of the feather itself. Keep in mind that there will always be greater definition at the ends of the tertial and tail feathers.

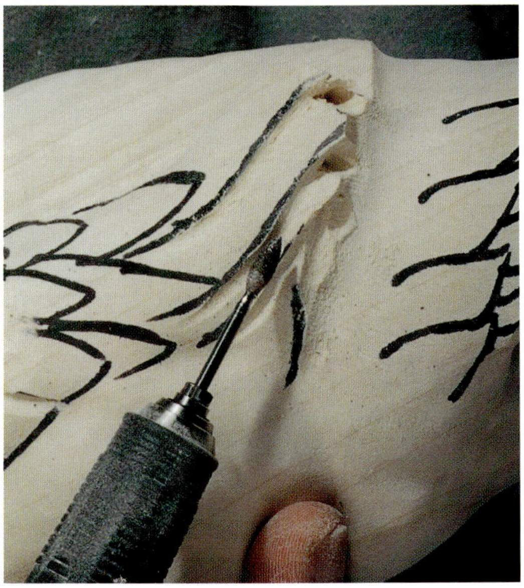

Here I am separating the tertial feathers. Again, note the greater definition of these feathers as compared to those on the back.

Prepare the sanded head for ruby work by drawing on the appropriate lines.

The rump and tail feathers are also defined with the ruby tool. Go ahead and complete the ruby work over the entire bird.

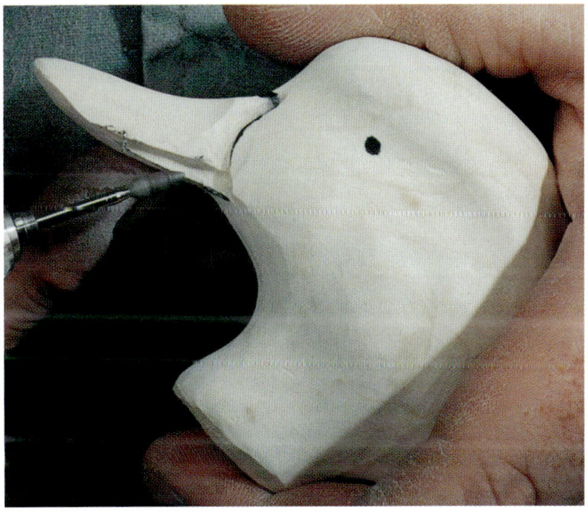

Use the ruby tool to define the edges of the bill.

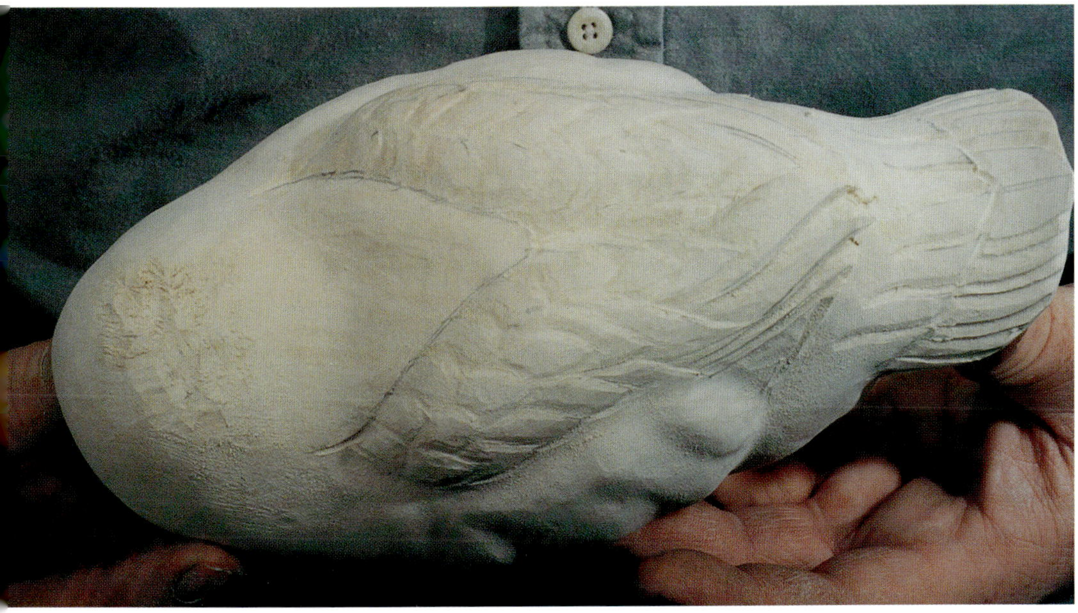

When you are finished defining all the feathers your bird should look like this.

Your drake head should look like this when you are done. For this head, I drilled the eyehole with a number 8mm eyebit, available through carving supply companies. The ruby tool can also be used to depress the eye hole.

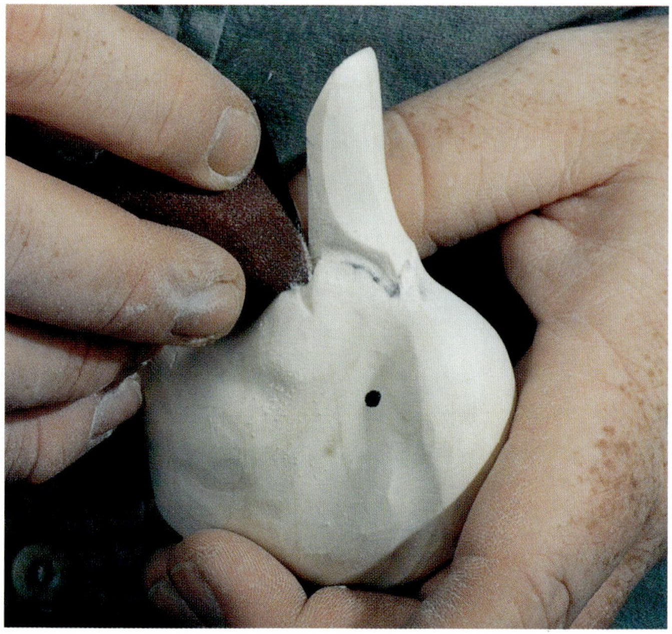

Use the folded sandpaper to sand around the grooves in the bill as well.

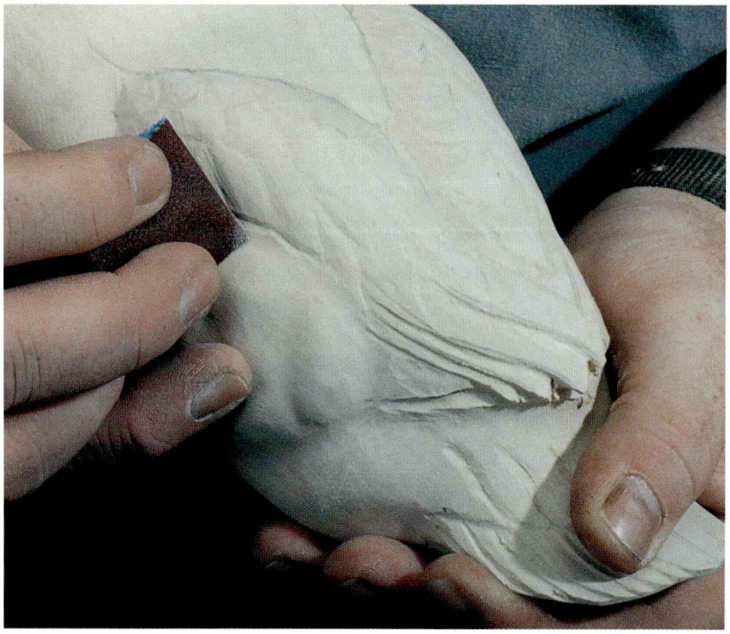

Hand sand the whole bird. I use 150 grit cloth backed paper, folding it to get into the tight grooves created by the ruby work.

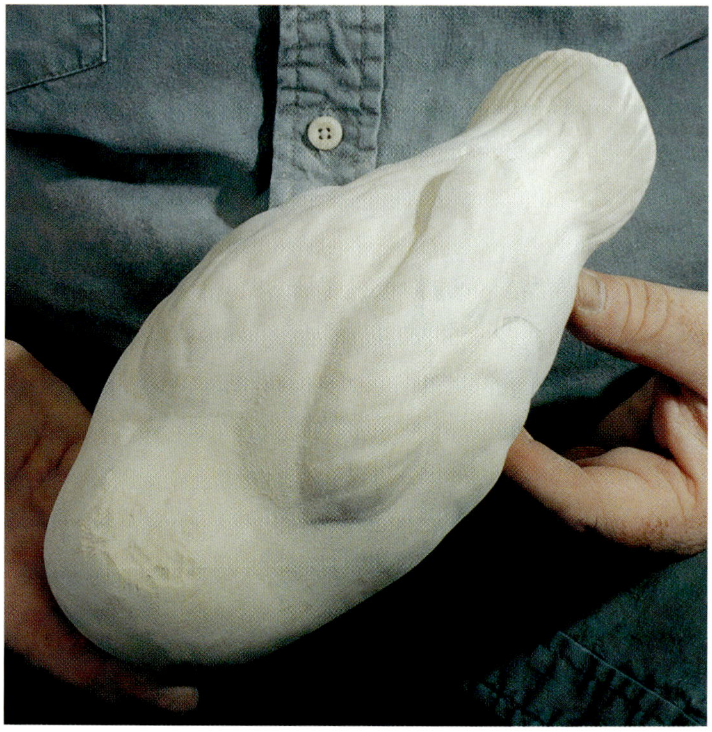

The finished, hand sanded bird.

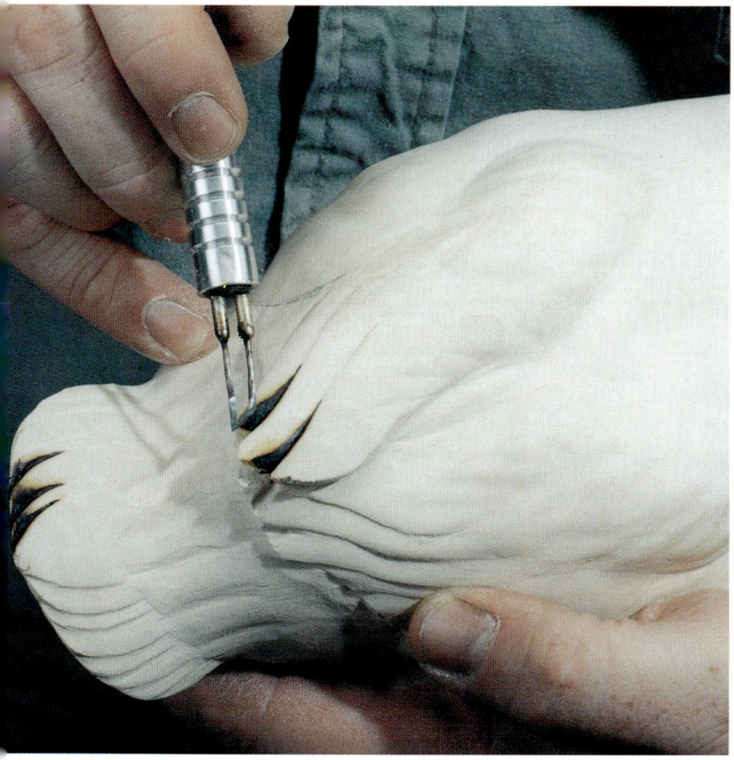

Using a burner, define the edges of the tertials, the tail feathers, and the outlines of the bill. I'm using a Detail Master III, 50 watt burning unit. Take your time — let the tool do the work for you and don't let it burn too hot. Remember you are using wood and you don't want to risk catching it on fire.

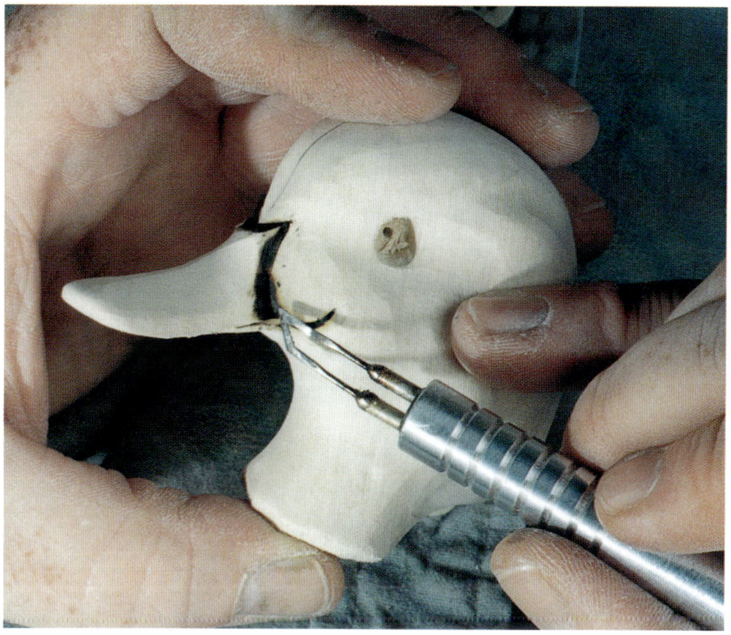

Use the burner to define the edges of the bill.

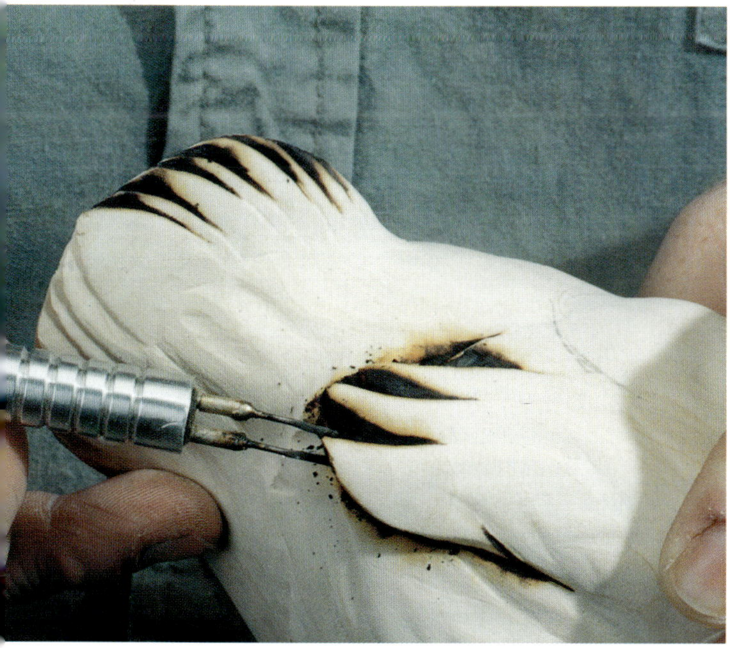

Progress. Hold the bird and burner out in front of you to avoid getting smoke in your eyes.

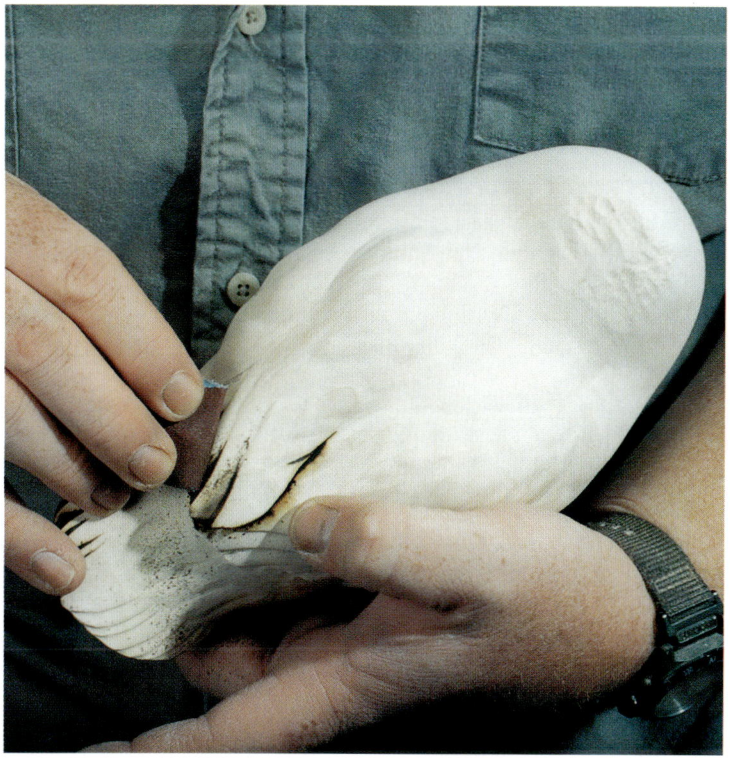

Using the 150 grit sandpaper, sand off any carbon residue created by the burner.

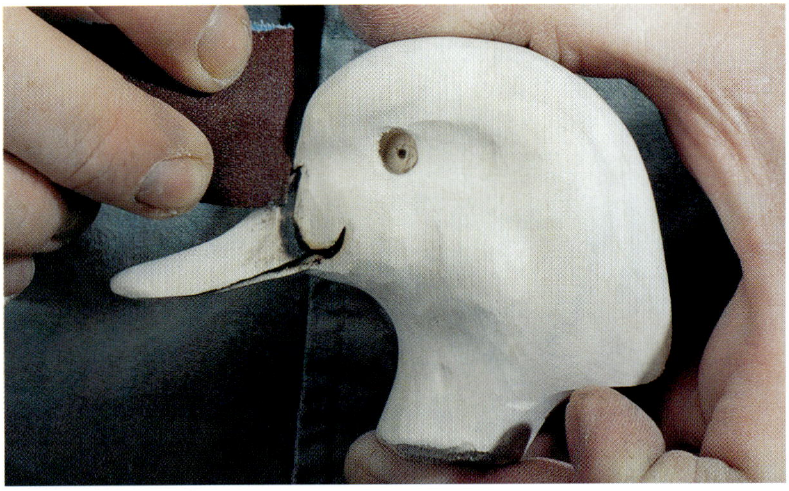

Sand any carbon off the bill as well.

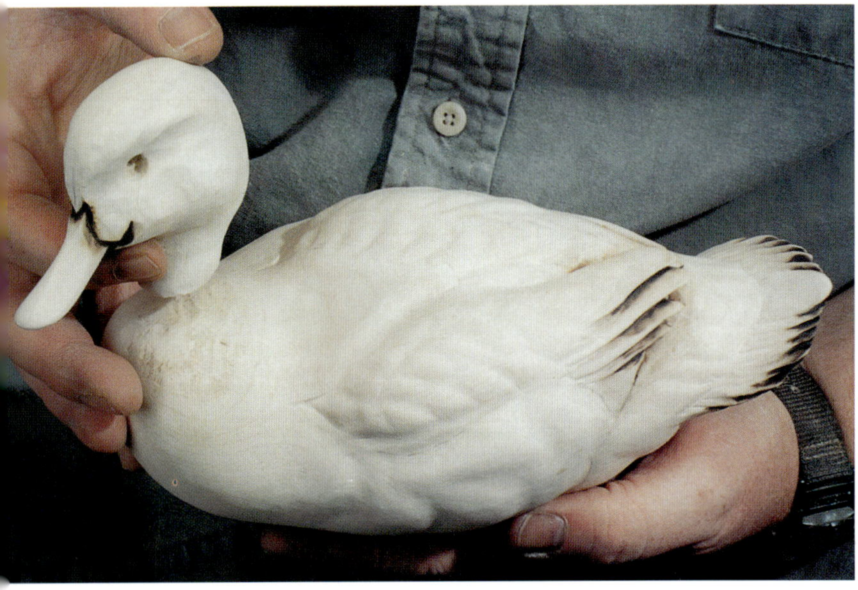

Hand sanding, tertial and tail feather definition, and bill definition have been completed on the drake.

The same steps completed on the hen.

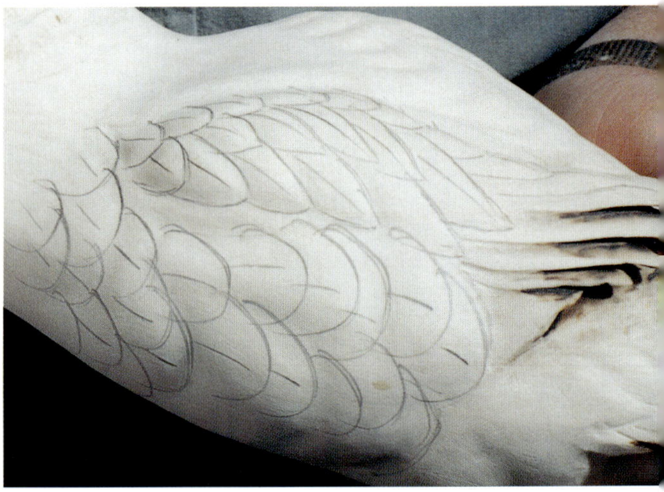

Burning the quills and individual feathers is next. Start by redrawing the feathers on the back and side of the bird.

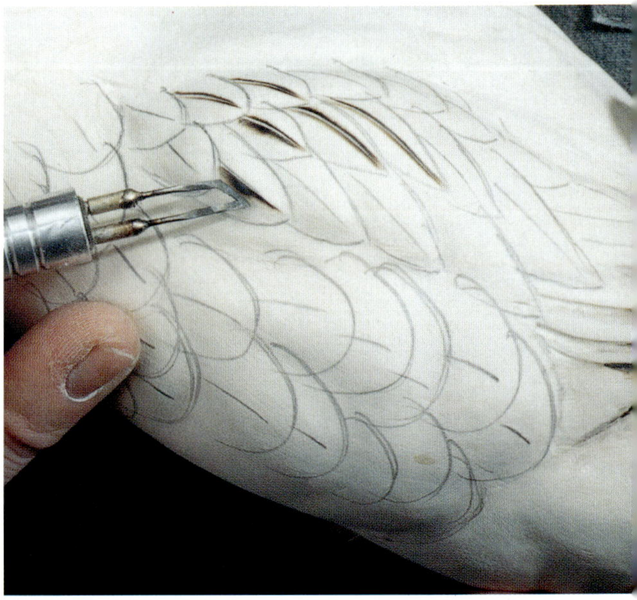

Lay the burner down along the lines to define the edges of the quills. Don't use it straight up and down or you won't get the definition you are after. Remember that the quill ends just before the tip of the feather.

The drake with all of the quills burned. Using a light touch with the burner is essential for this step.

Using a pencil, draw lines where the splits on each feather will be carved in with the ruby. Variance is the key to realism: some splits should be longer, some shorter. Be sure that each feather is different than the next.

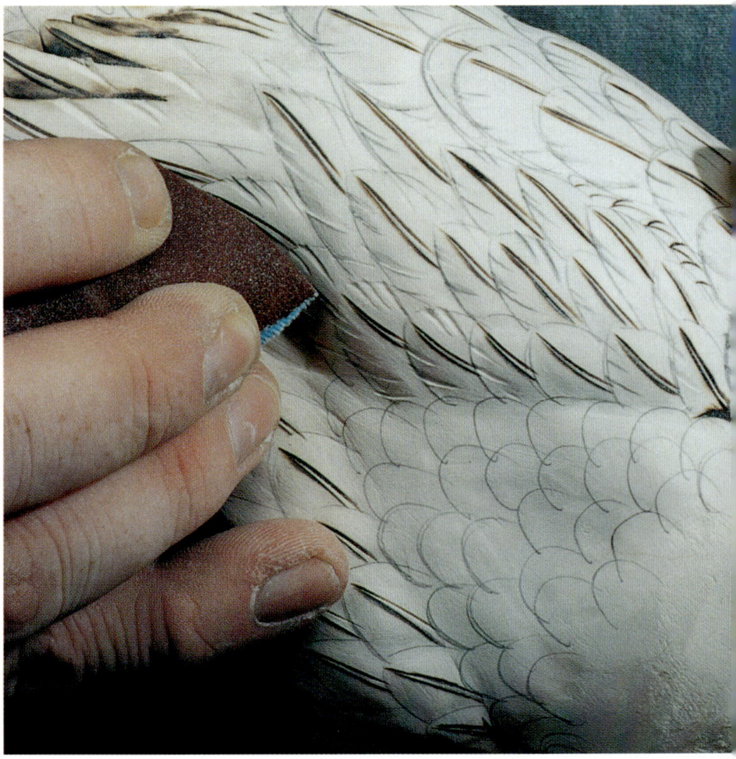

Following any ruby work, sanding is necessary. Fold the paper on a crisp edge and sand lightly right in the groove of the split.

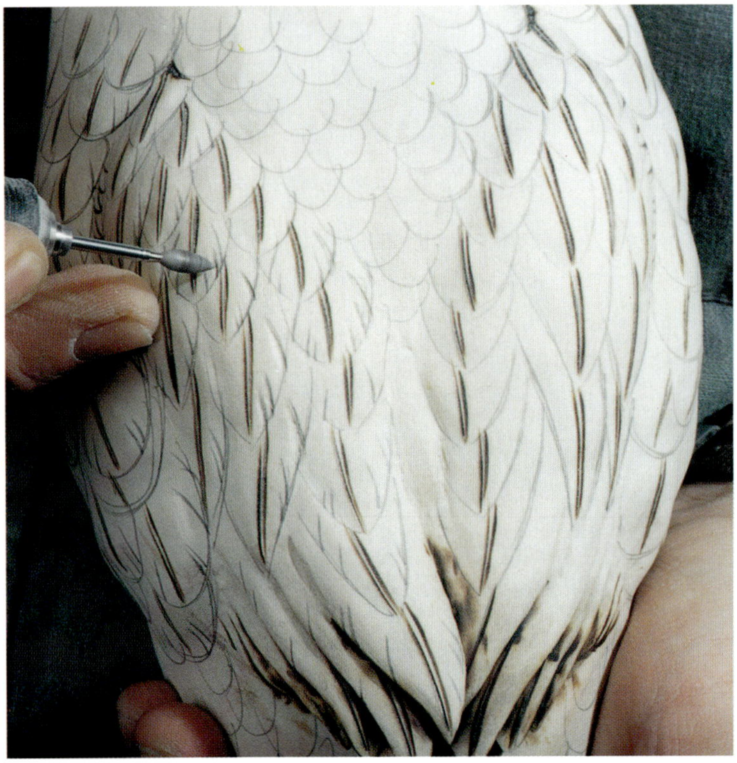

Use the point of the ruby to go right along the pencil edge, always rounding the wood towards the inside (i.e., *towards* the quill). Remember to vary the length and widths of the splits.

Creases in between feathers are good places to show some depth. I've shaded in the areas here that I will depress with the ruby.

The bird after several splits have been carved into the feathers.

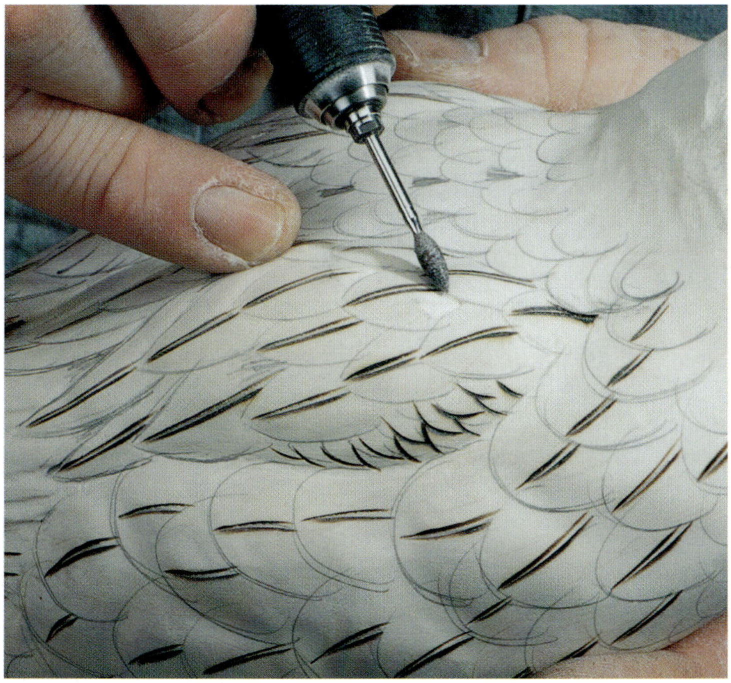

I'm pointing to one of the shaded areas that I've carved with the ruby.

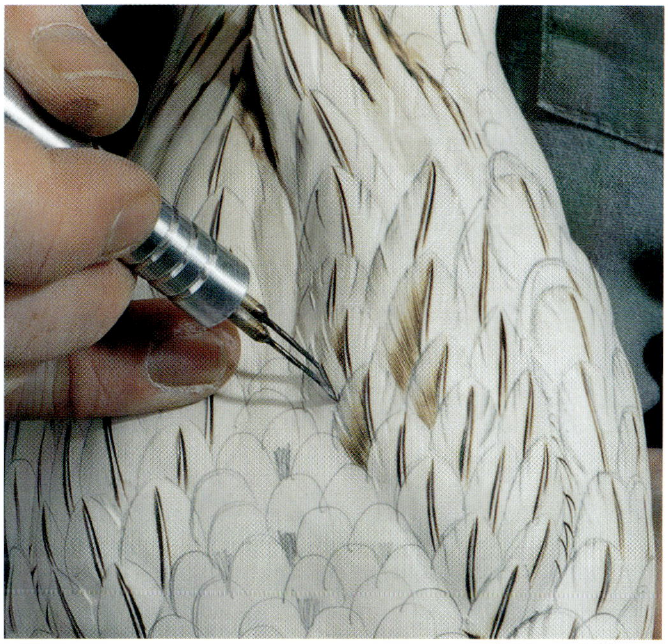

Using the burner, make fine lines in the opposite direction (i.e., from the quill towards the edge), keeping the interior of the feather much softer than the edges. Here I have completed this step on one side of three feathers. Go ahead and complete this for all of them.

Use an aluminum oxide white stone to create the ragged edges of the feather (when I start with a new stone, I turn the machine up full speed and use a piece of sandpaper to work off any burrs or rough areas). Holding the tool like a pencil, make multiple pulls from the edge of the feather towards the quill, remembering that the stone should only come midway through the feather. Aim for a coarser texture on the edge of the feather than in the center.

Small rounded feathers are now drawn on the rump and chest to complete the layout.

Using the stone, make multiple strokes from the outside edge of the feathers towards the center, creating their texture. For these smaller feathers, the stone is enough to create the needed texture — they don't need to be burned in addition.

The drake after all the stoning and burning have been completed on the feathers.

This view shows the underside of the tail and rump.

The hen with the same steps completed will look like this.

Now back to our head. Draw in the lines for the nostril, the mustache . . .

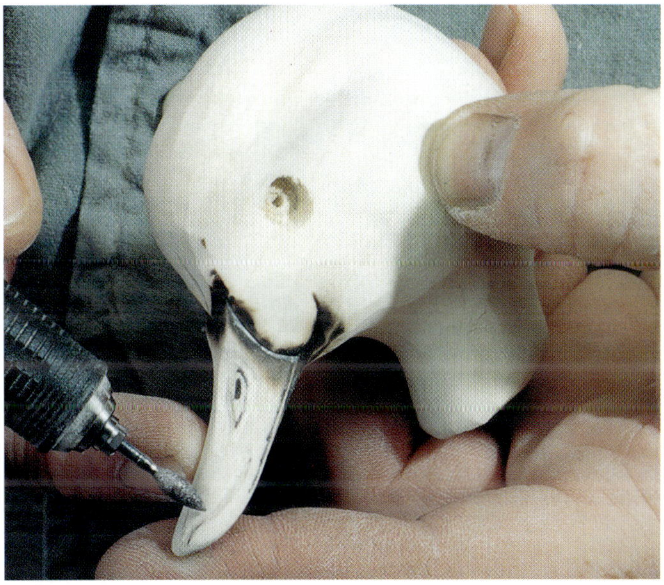

Use the ruby to go around all the lines you drew. Here is the top of the bill in progress . . .

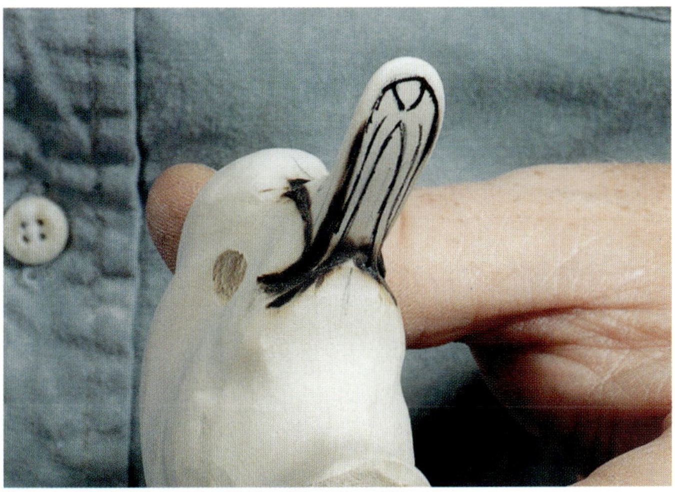

. . . and the tendon that contracts to open the lower mandible. Again, I've used a marker to make it easier to see; normally I use pencil for drawing these lines.

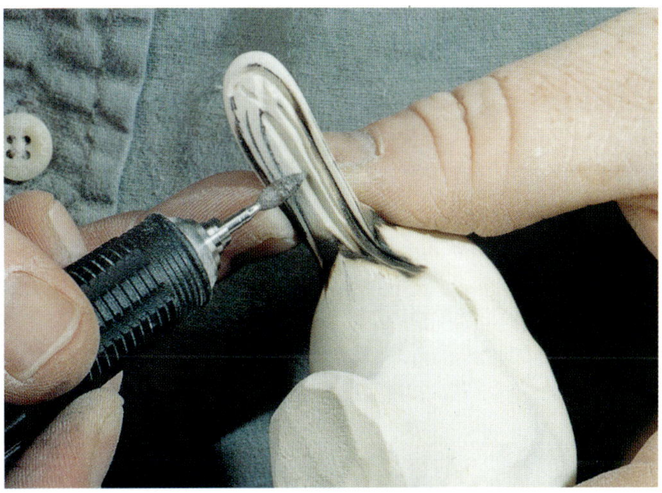

. . . and the bottom.

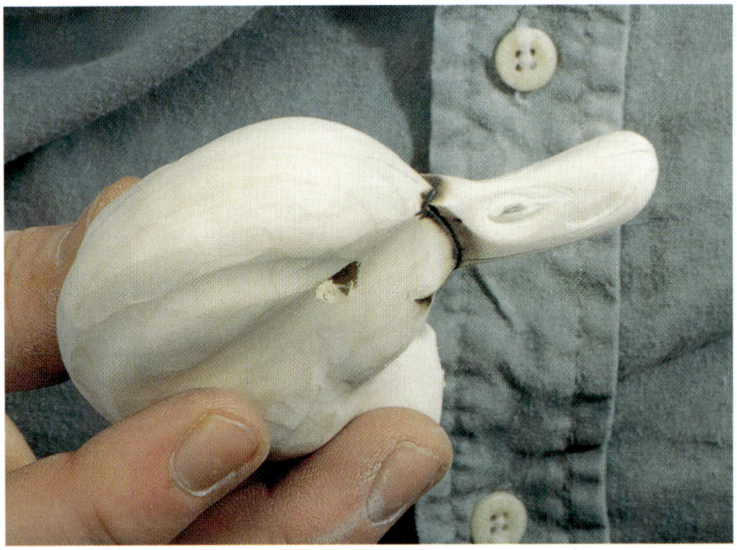

The ruby work has been completed on the bill.

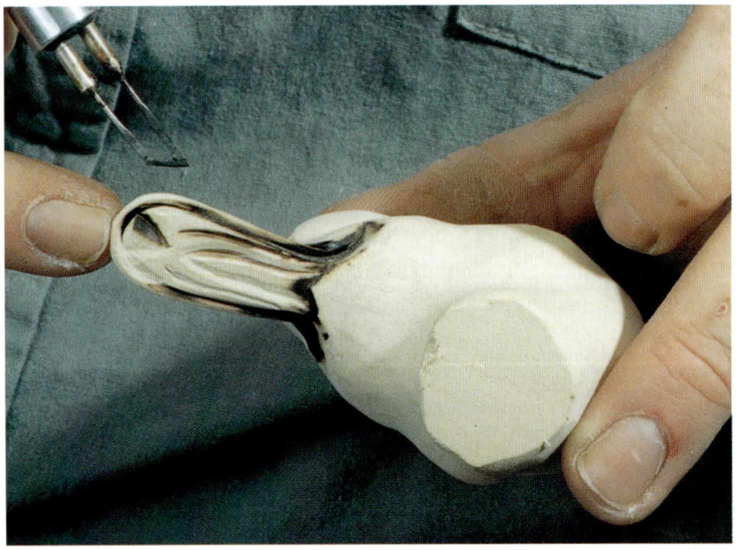

Use the burner to crisp up the lines on the bill. Here I am doing the underside.

Here is the top of the bill with the burning completed . . .

. . . and the bottom.

Draw pencil lines to represent the direction of the feather flow on the head.

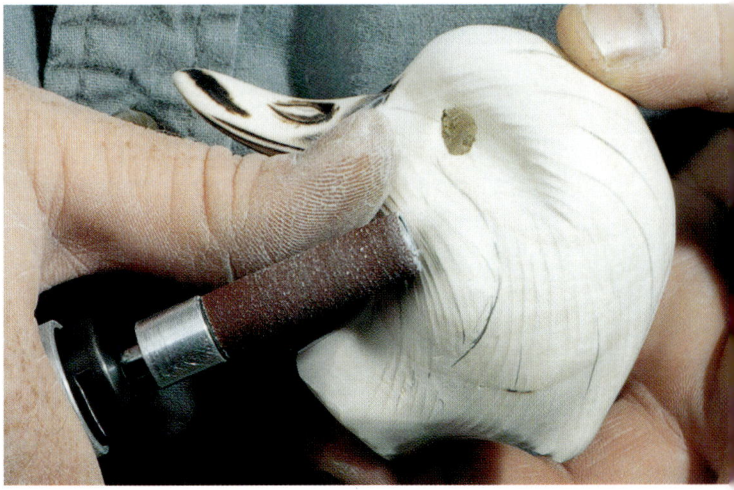

Use the sponge sander on the same areas to create highs and lows for the feather flow.

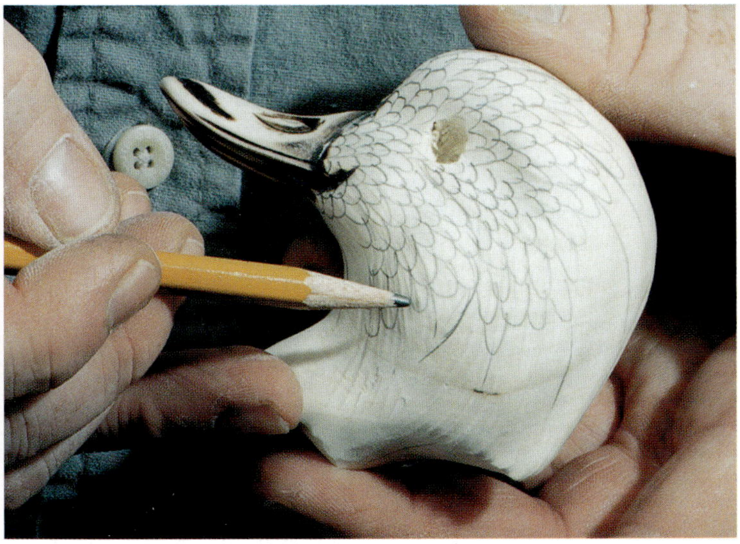

Draw in all the small feathers on the head.

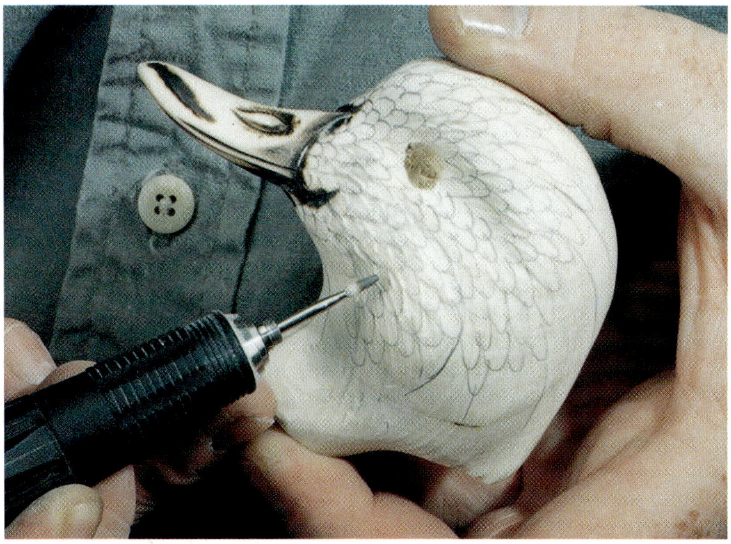

Use the same size stone as before to texture the head feathers. The key is to use short, light strokes for this process.

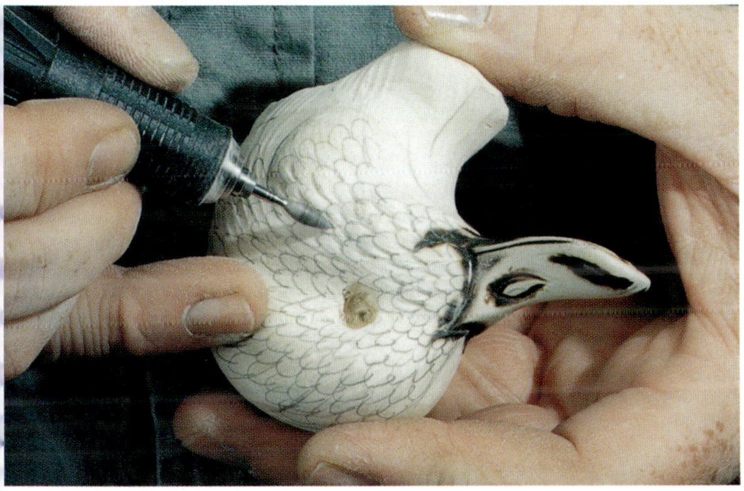

Using the ruby, very lightly depress the interior of each feather.

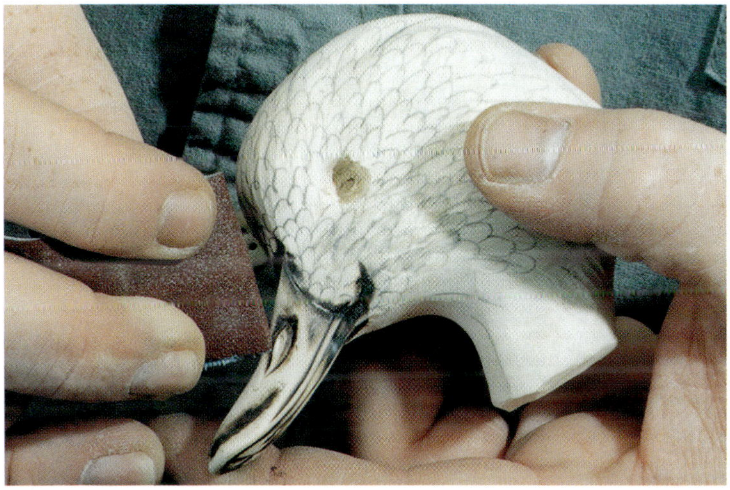

This is a good time to sand the char off the bill that was created with the burning.

Depress each nostril on the top of the bill as well. Use the ruby along the center line you drew before.

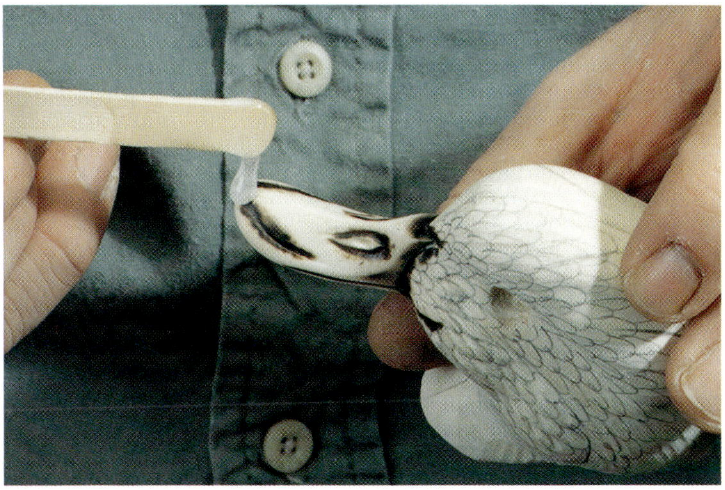

To create the nail on the tip of the bill, mix equal parts of 5 minute epoxy and drop a small amount on the tip of the bill. Keep turning the head straight up and straight down as the bead dries to keep it from dripping off.

After the bead has dried, use the burner to create the wrinkles in the bill.

To glue the drake's head onto the body, mix equal parts of 5 minute epoxy and put a small amount on the chest area and on the neck. Wait about four minutes until it gets tacky, then position the head on the body. I like to turn it slightly to the side for more realism.

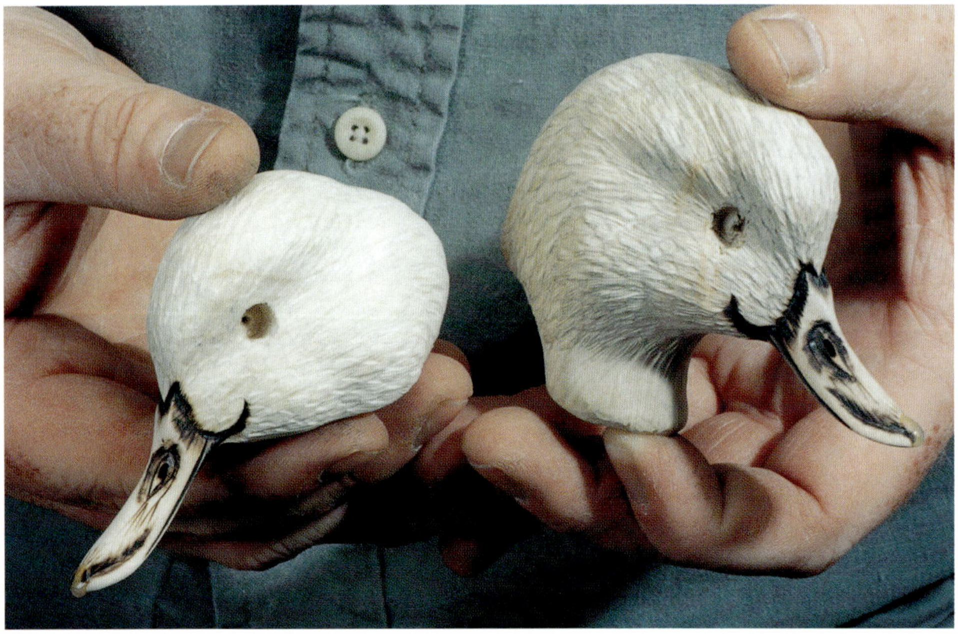

The carving is completed on the head. Here is the hen on the left and the drake on the right.

Auto body filler (Bondo is most common brand) is used to hide the seam between the head and the body. Apply the auto body at least 1/2" above the top and bottom of the seam; the depth of the layer should also be about 1/2". Let dry a good ten minutes before proceeding to the next step.

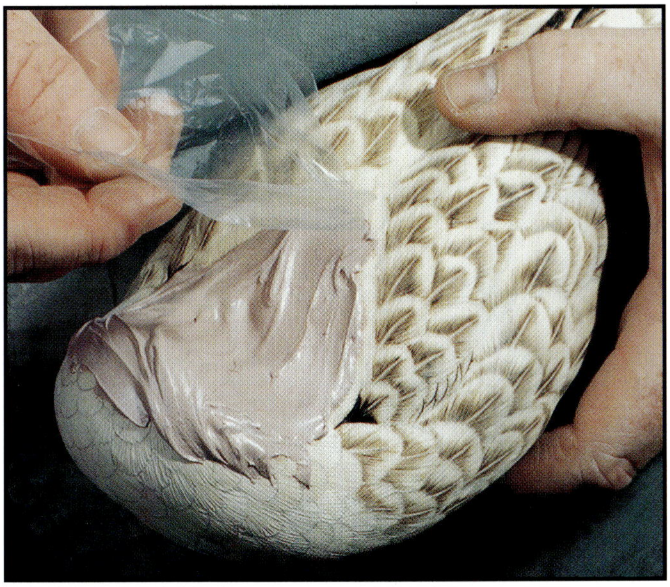

The hen's head will not be attached until after it has been painted. For now, spread auto body in the pocket where the head is going to rest then cover it with a very thin plastic bag

Set the hen's head on top of the plastic so it creates a mold of the head for a perfect seam.

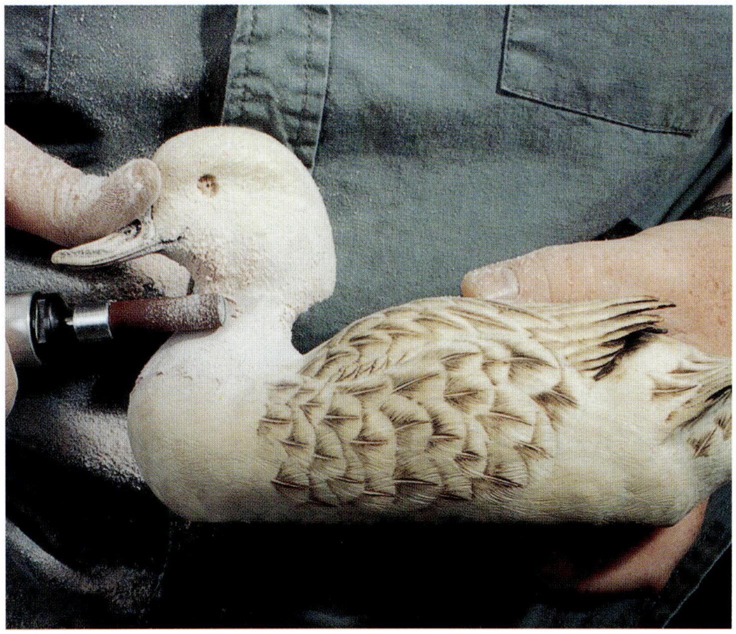

Back to the drake. Sand the auto body layer around the neck using the sponge sander. A mask and goggles should always be used during this sanding.

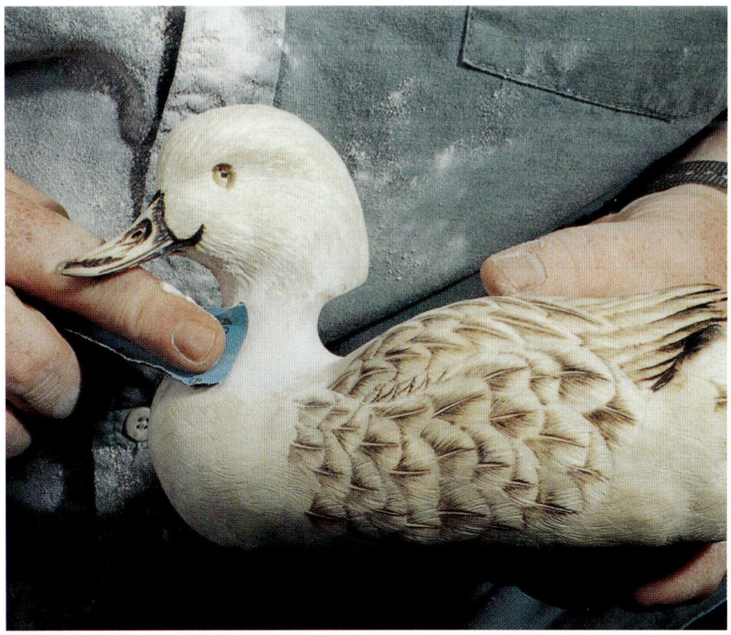

Finish with some hand sanding to smooth the seam completely.

The auto body will be carved and painted just like the rest of the bird. Start by drawing in the remaining neck and chest feathers with a pencil.

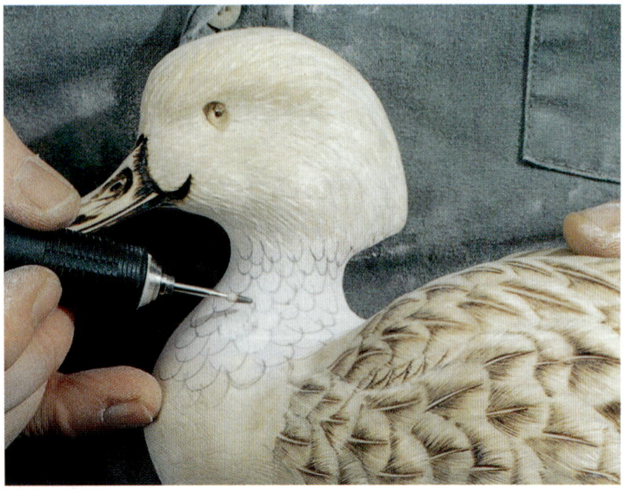

Using the same stone as before, texture these feathers just as you did on the head and chest.

When you are done sanding and texturizing the neck, your drake should look like this.

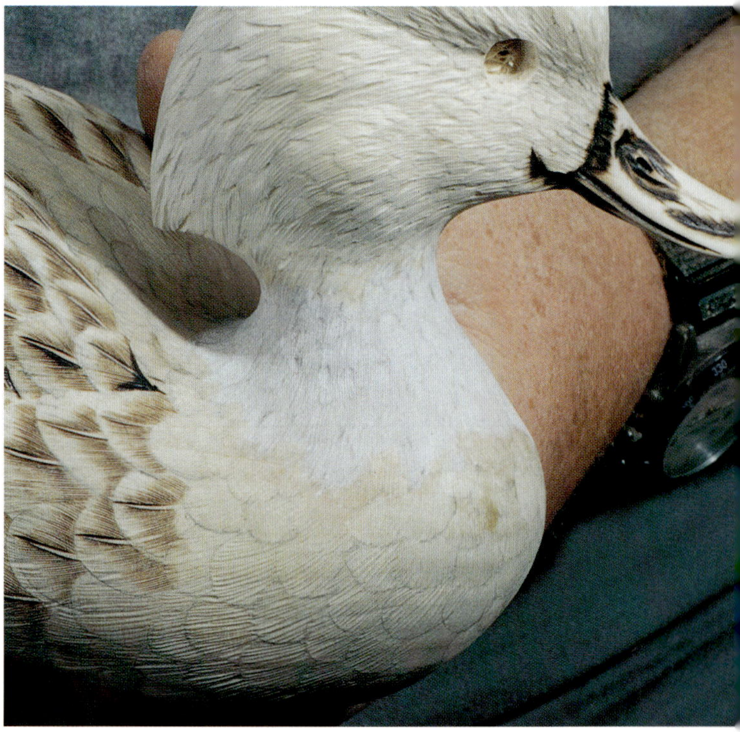

A close-up view of the drake's neck area.

Here is the hen at the same point in the process — headless, of course!

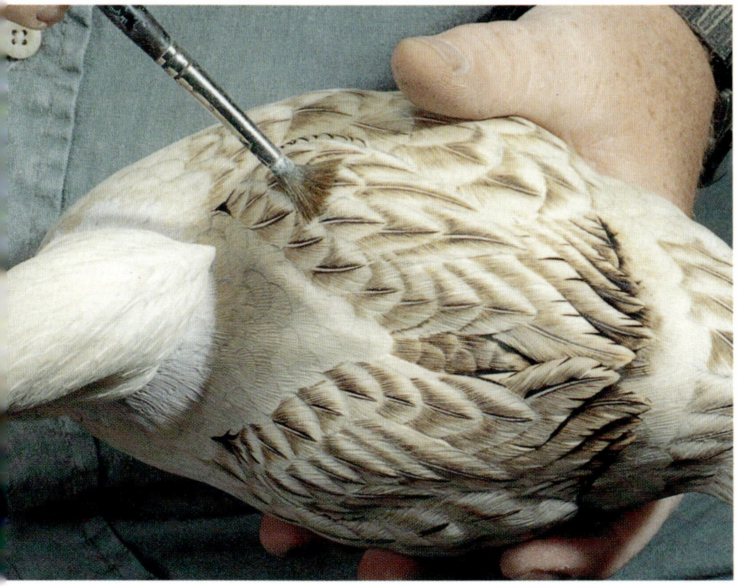

In preparation for sealing, clean off all the dust that has accumulated on the bird. A toothbrush or paintbrush works well for this.

A close-up of the drake's head after sealing.

Apply three coats of sealer to the bird, allowing time to dry between coats. I find lacquer based wood sealers to be the best, with enamel based running a close second. If using the lacquer based sealer always thin it according to the instructions on the can. Here is the drake after three coats of sealer have been applied.

The hen with the sealer applied.

We will add 8mm enamel back brown eyes next. You can get these from a variety of craft stores or catalogs.

Cut equal amounts of the resin and hardener. Mix thoroughly and knead them together. When mixed together properly, all putties will become a solid color. Wash your hands very well after mixing the putty to avoid getting any putty on the bird itself.

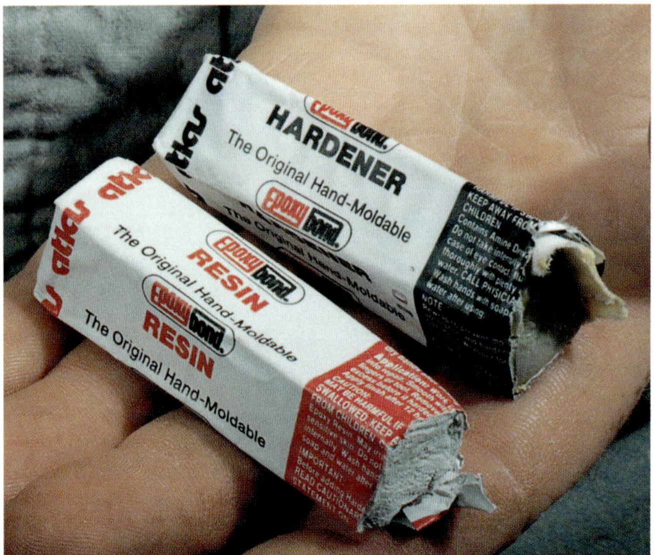

I use plumber's putty to attach the eyes. It will get hard as a rock. I use Atlas brand, but any putty will do.

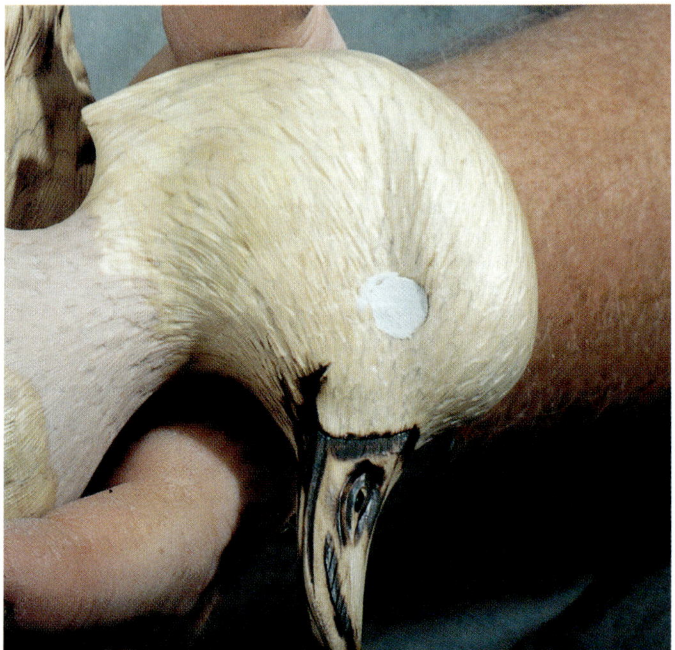

Take a small amount of putty and fill the eye hole flush to the rim.

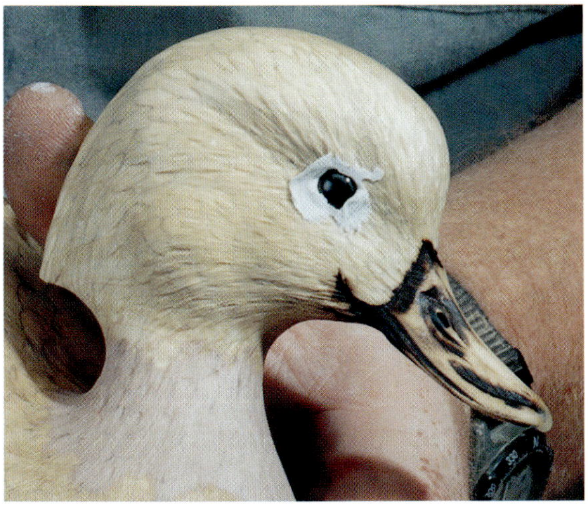

Place the eye on top of the putty and push it in to the proper depth. If your depth is correct, you should be able to see just a tiny amount of the eye when the bird is viewed straight down from the top of the head.

Use a damp finger to smooth out the putty remaining around the eye. Pull the putty into the edges of the feathers until it is as smooth as possible.

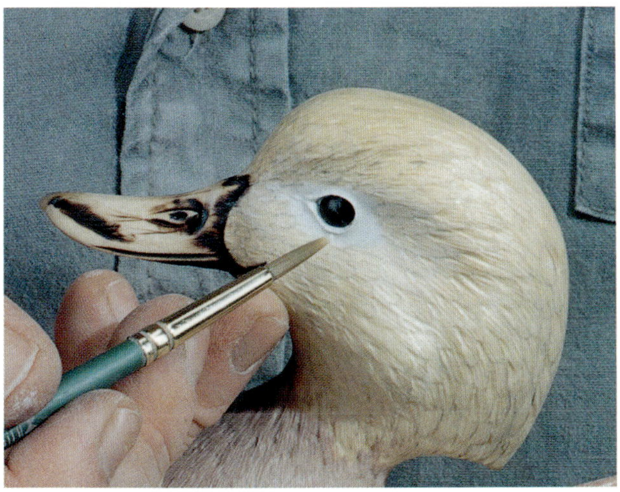

With a moist paintbrush, gently push on the putty that encircles the eye, building it up to create an eyelid. The eye should be egg shaped, larger and rounder in the back and more tapered in the front. Complete this step for both eyes.

The initial steps for the hen's eyes are the same as for the drake. However, we are going to give her a half closed eye. Place a small amount of putty on your fingertip . . .

. . . and smooth it onto the lower part of the eye to create the half closed eyelid.

Use the moist paintbrush again to create a tiny bit of depth between the eye and the eyelid, at both the top and bottom.

The hen's eye completed.

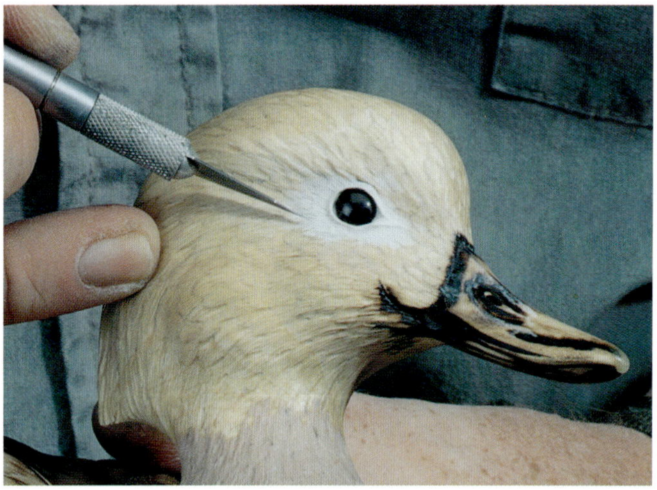

Using a damp X-Acto™ knife blade, add some texture to the putty. You want to match the feather texture of the surrounding head, blending the putty nicely into it.

This is a good time to check over the bird's body for any nicks, cracks, or airholes that need to be filled in with putty. The putty needs to dry at least overnight before you begin painting.

The same process is completed for the hen's head.

Let's begin carving the primaries. These have been cut about 1/4" thick out of tupelo.

Start by rounding each side of the primaries with the sponge sander.

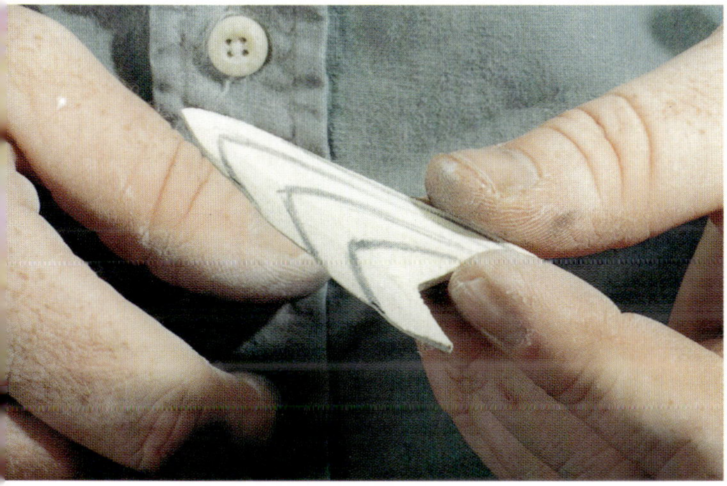

Draw in the lines for the feathers.

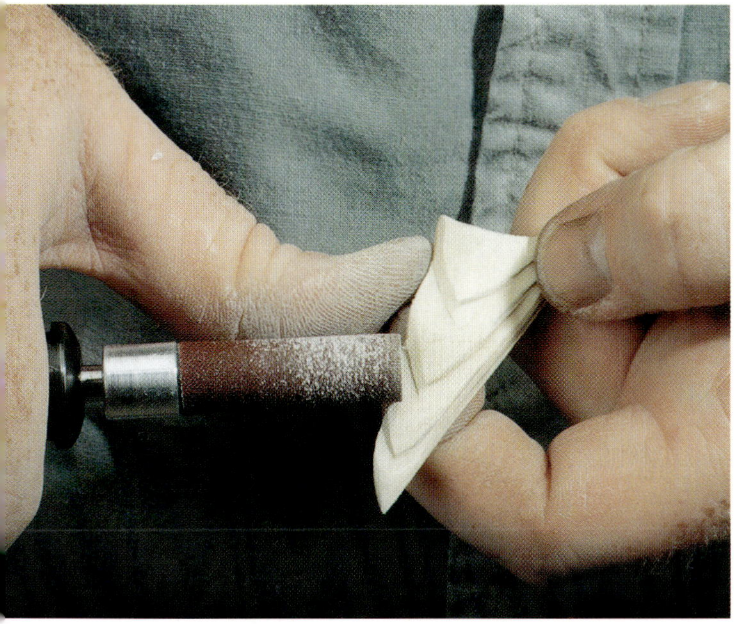

Use the sponge sander on the lines to create the individual feather definition of the primaries.

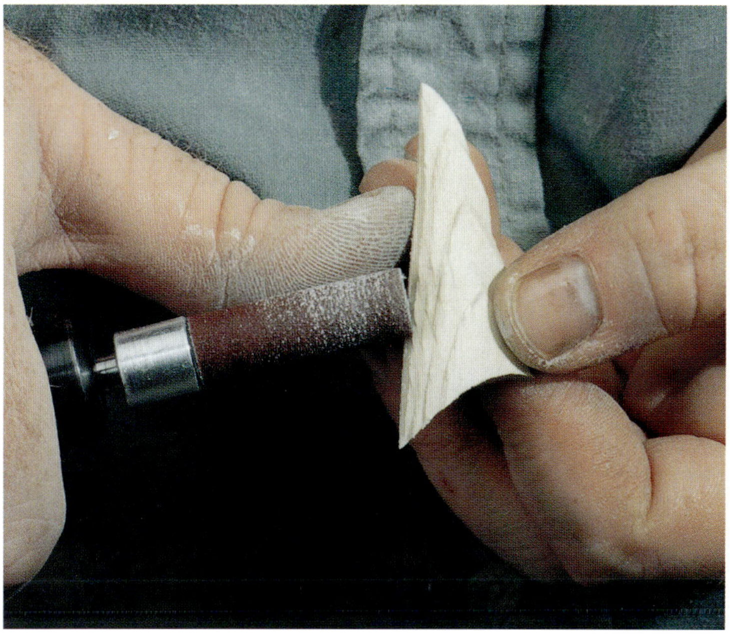

Lightly texture the edges of the primaries.

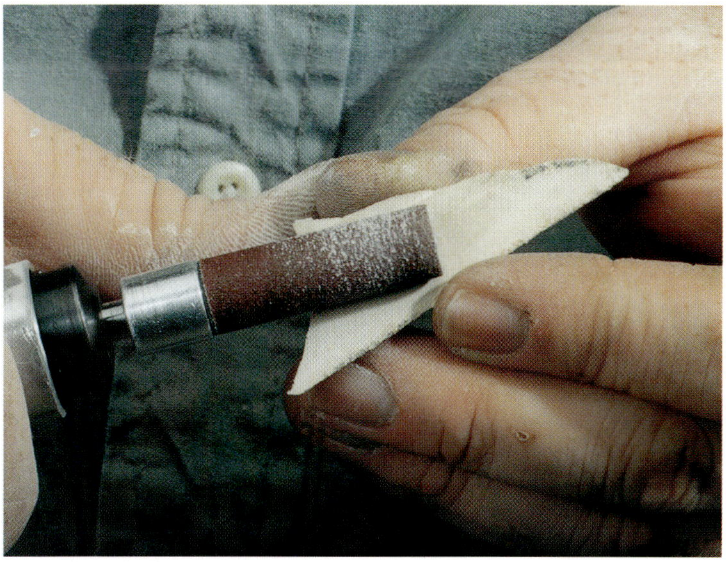

Still using the sponge sander, create a concave surface on the bottom of each primary.

Draw the quill lines in preparation for burning.

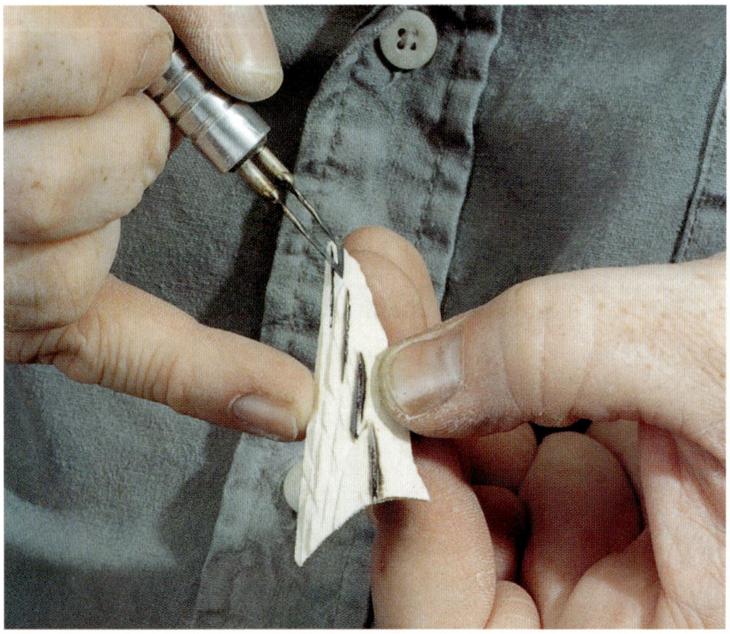

Burn the quill lines very lightly, just as you did on the body of the bird.

Now use the burner to create the individual barbs.

When you have completed burning the quills and barbs, the primaries should look like this.

On the underside of the primaries, the edges have been burned and then stoned to add texture.

In preparation for painting, coat the entire bird (other than the eyes) with gesso, a primer known for its adhesive qualities. (The sealer we used on the bird would prevent any water based acyrlic paint from adhering well if we did not use the gesso.) Although gesso used to be sold only in white, several colors are now available. I prefer the colored gesso since I have to apply less paint to cover it later. Before starting, thin the gesso with water to a thick cream consistency — about 40% water to 60% gesso. One to two medium coats will work better than several thin washes.

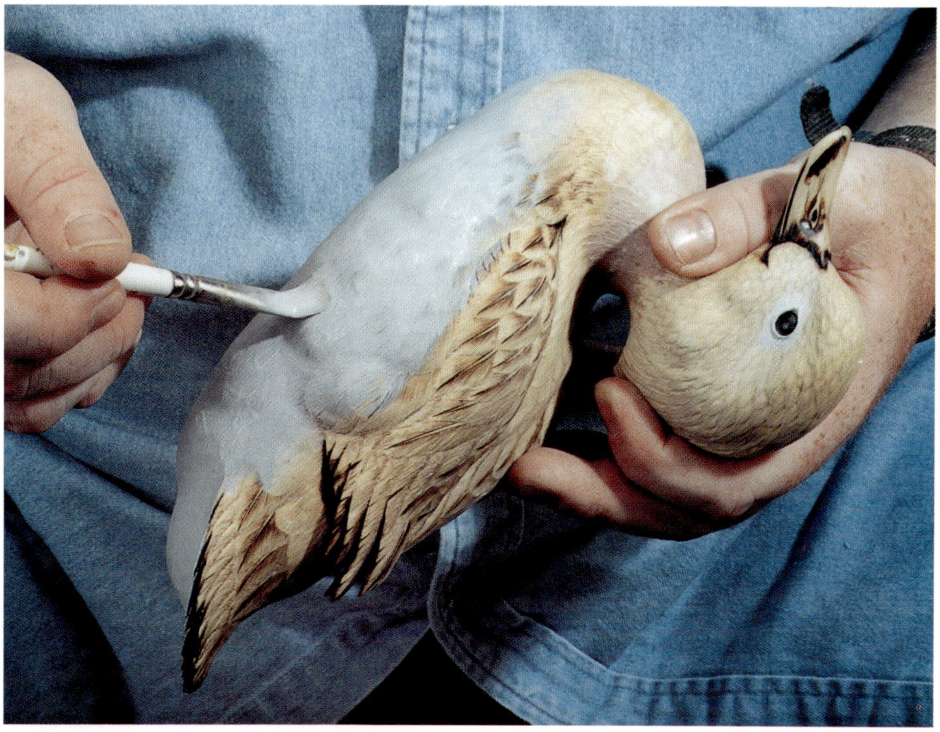

Gray gesso works well for the drake. Coat the head and all lower portions first so you can still hold the bird on top, then place on a table to finish the back. (You don't need to do the flat underside of the bird.) Use your brush to work over any air bubbles that may appear as you are applying the gesso. Avoid getting gesso on the eye; it will be very difficult to remove and you risk chipping the glass in the process. Let the gesso dry thoroughly then apply a second coat.

The completed gessoed drake.

White gesso tinted with a very small amount of raw sienna paint is used for the hen's head, lower portion, and underrump.

Applying white gesso to the lower portion of the hen.

Here's a handy tip: before you start, drill a small hole in the bottom of the hen's head so you can insert a pencil to hold the head while you are applying the gesso.

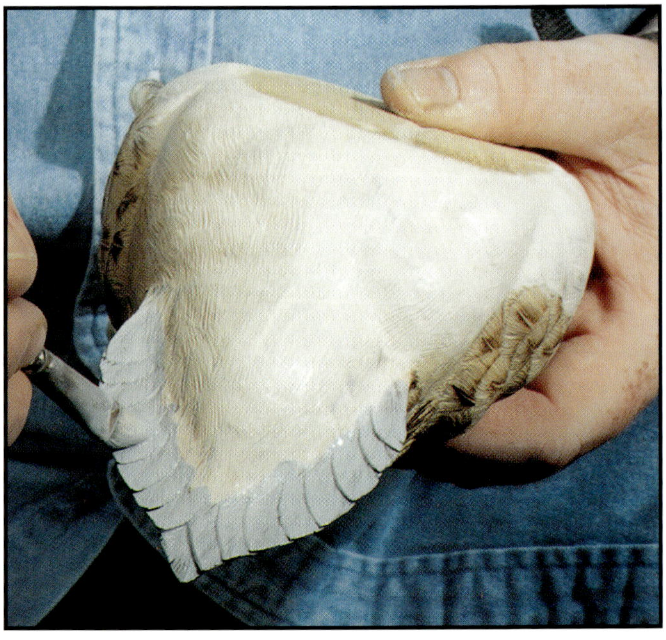

Apply gray gesso to the underside of the hen's tail feathers.

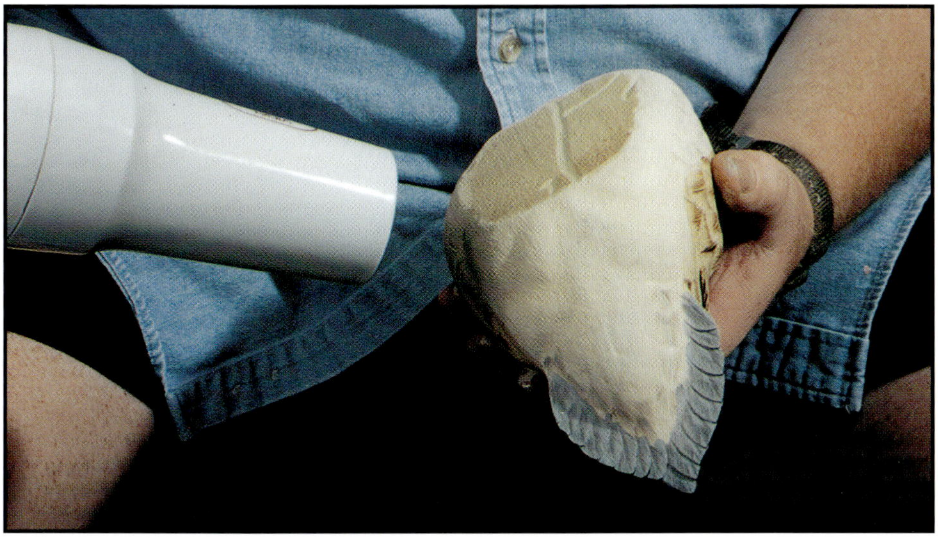

A hair dryer can be used to speed up the drying process.

Apply brown gesso to the rest of the hen, covering both the auto body and the wood. Let dry thoroughly, then apply a second coat.

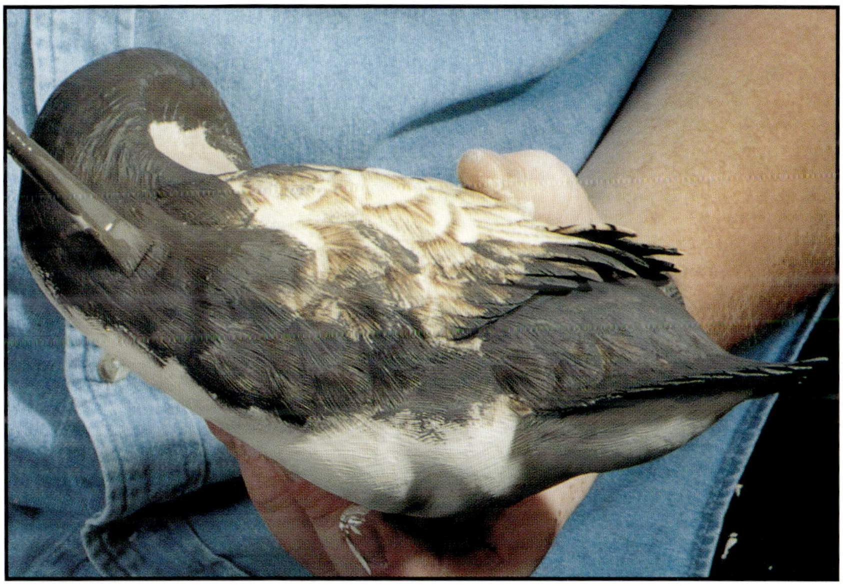

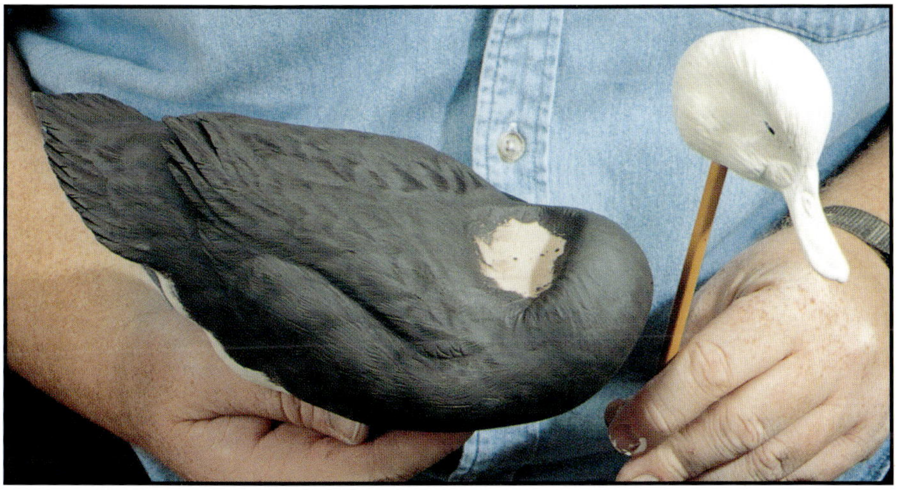

The completed gessoed hen.

Painting

Airbrushing the Drake

Prior to airbrushing, we will block out some initial colors on the drake. Start with burnt sienna acrylic, thinned with water to a thick cream consistency. Apply this to the top and cheek area of the head on both sides. The acrylic needs to dry for approximately fifteen minutes before applying any paint to the same area. Again, a hair dyer can be used to speed up the drying time.

Apply yellow oxide to each side of the underrump in a teardrop shape.

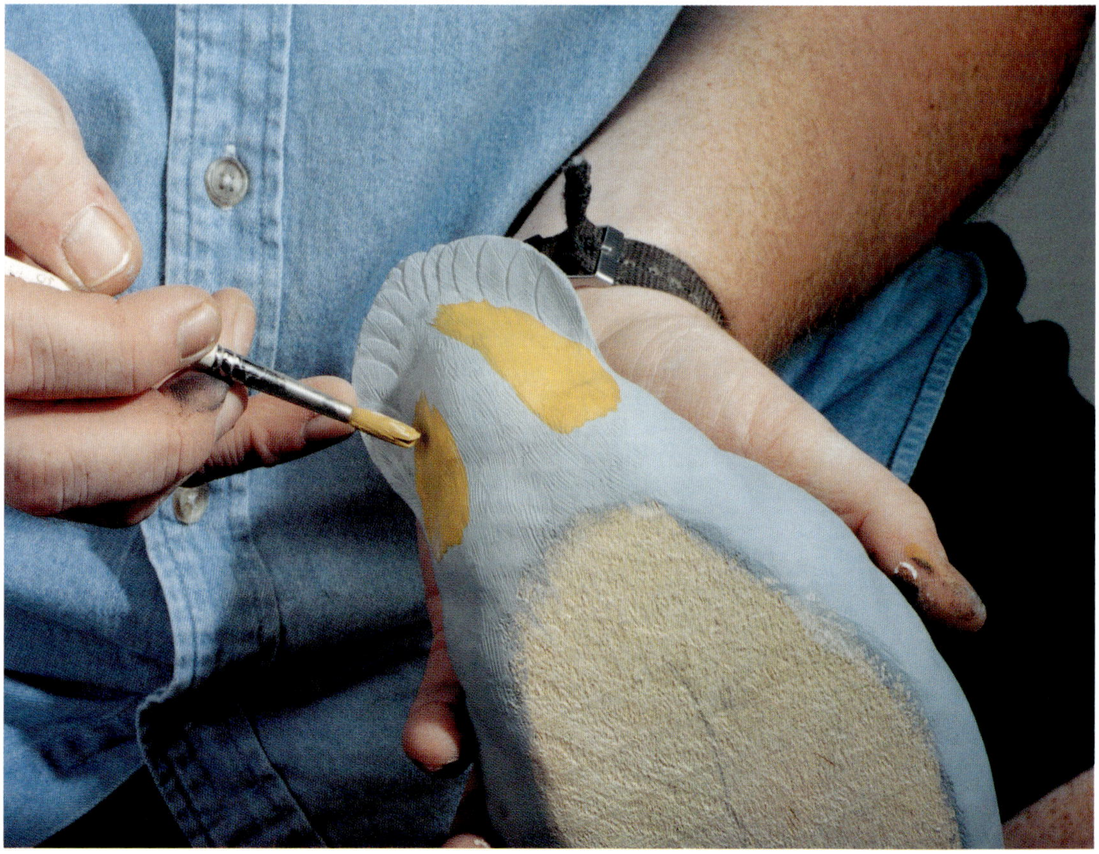

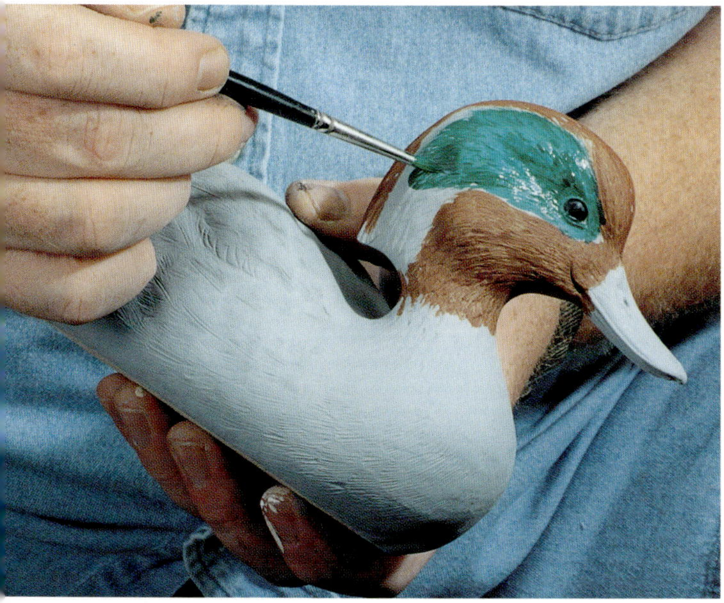

Use thalo green to coat the iridescent patch behind the drake's eye.

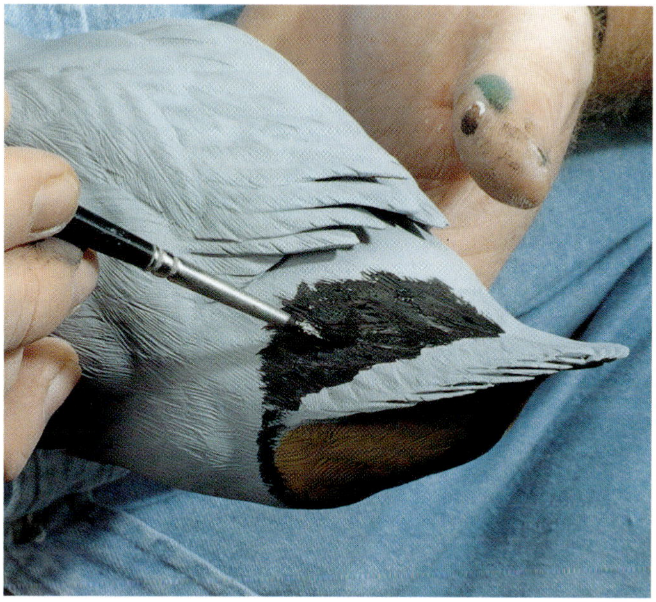

Above and below: Use black to define areas of the upper and lower rump. Now go over the burnt sienna, yellow oxide, thalo green, and black with a second coat.

The drake's head to this point.

The blocking is completed and we are ready to airbrush. I like small plastic condiment cups like this for thinning the paint. Add a small amount of water to the paint and mix with a brush (don't use a popsicle stick as it won't break up the paint enough). Be careful not to make the paint too thin — aim for a thick cream consistency. Prepare all your most common colors in advance so you won't be slowed down once you start painting.

Hold the bird with the tail away from you. Using straight white, shoot the center of the side feathers in order to lighten the interior of each feather. Make sure the paint mists towards the rear of the bird.

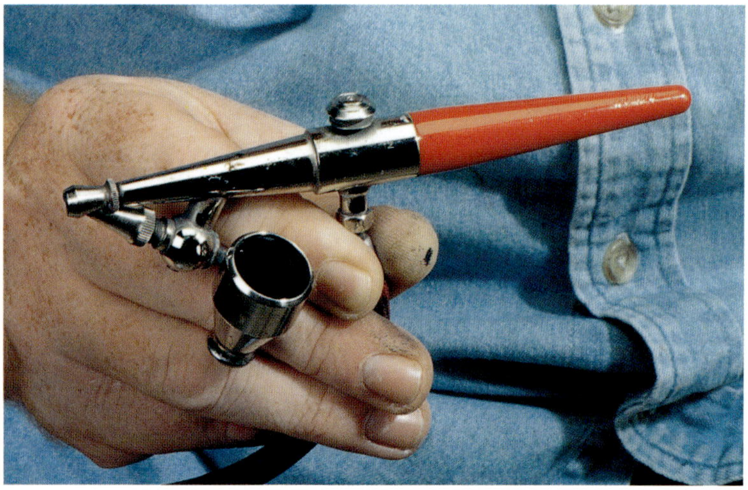

I will be using a Pasche H single action airbrush, by far the simplest airbrush to use. Air pressure should be at about 40 pounds — that's a little higher than recommended, but makes for a much softer job. Your paint should also be a little thicker than generally recommended. As a rule of thumb, spray the lighter colors first. This is because any overspray with the lighter colors tends to show up much more than with the darker colors. Practice on a piece of cardboard until you get the technique down and learn how to direct the paint: the closer you hold the gun the more intense and solid your spray will be; the further away the gun, the more misted the spray.

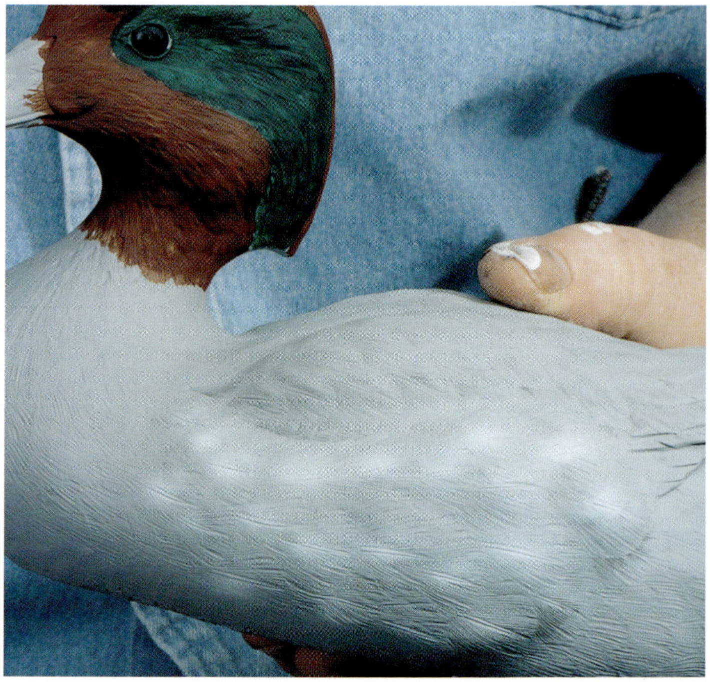

This step completed.

Now spray a little white on the underside, at the tip of the yellow markings.

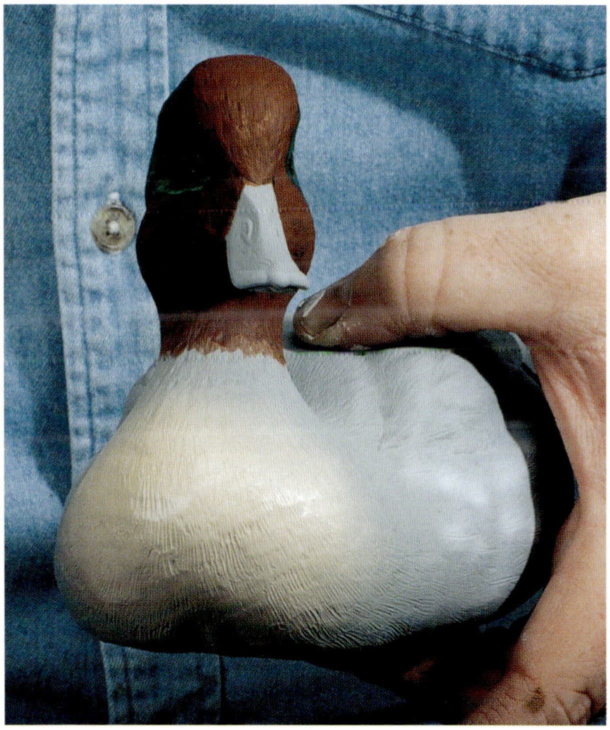

The chest area to this point.

Use a combination of 70% white, 15% raw sienna, and 15% burnt sienna to spray the drake's chest area. Keeping your gun clean in between colors is very important. Open the head up completely and let water run through it, then spray the head with an all purpose cleaner like 409.

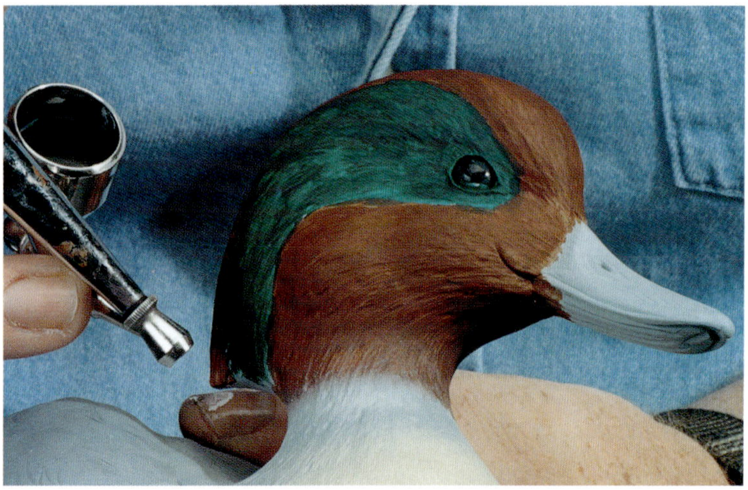

Use some gray to touch up around the neck.

Gray is also used to add a little softness around the black saddle.

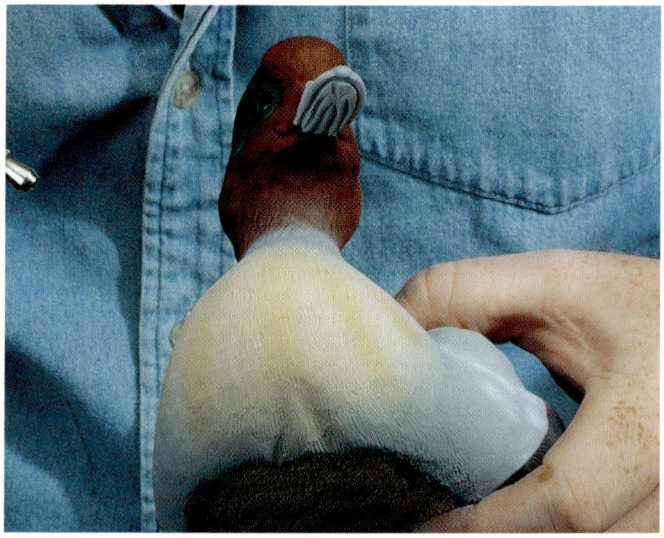

Mist raw sienna on the chest.

Mist raw sienna on the top of the cheeks as well.

Mix two thirds burnt umber and one third raw sienna to get a "hen brown" color. Use this to mist the interior of all the back feathers and the cape.

Continue spraying raw sienna around the top of the iridescent green patch. The green patch is now outlined with raw sienna.

Using hen brown, haze the top of the tail feathers, misting from the tip and fading back towards the rump feathers. The color should be most intense at the very edges.

Spray raw sienna at the base of the yellow underrump markings.

Use the same technique on the underside of the tail feathers.

I have completed the back feathers, tail feathers, and cape with the hen brown.

Lightly outline the lower half of the ball feathers with the hen brown. This gives the bird some added depth.

Add a little iridescent red or maroon to your burnt sienna and lightly mist this over the burnt sienna areas already done on the head. When using powdered iridescence, your acrylic paints need to be a little thinner than usual (otherwise the powdered color will clog up the gun).

Chroma™ makes some fabulous iridescent colors for the gun — I will use their iridescent green next. This color is airbrush ready, no thinning is required. Spray the iridescent green over the existing green patch on the head.

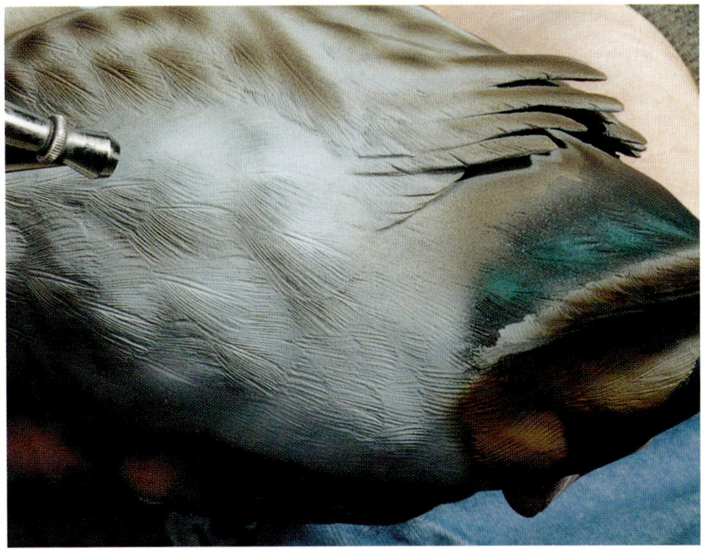

Use the same iridescent green on the interior of the upper rump feathers. As you hold the bird, make sure you constantly check your fingers to be sure you are not picking up paint from anywhere and inadvertently getting it on the bird.

Now mix the iridescent green with cadmium yellow to make a lighter iridescent green, almost a lime iridescent green. Spray this on the high points of the green patch on the head . . .

. . . and the middle of the upper rump feathers.

The drake so far.

Straight burnt umber will be used on the top of the head, to make a few dots on the chest, and for the center of each feather on the back. Top of the head is first.

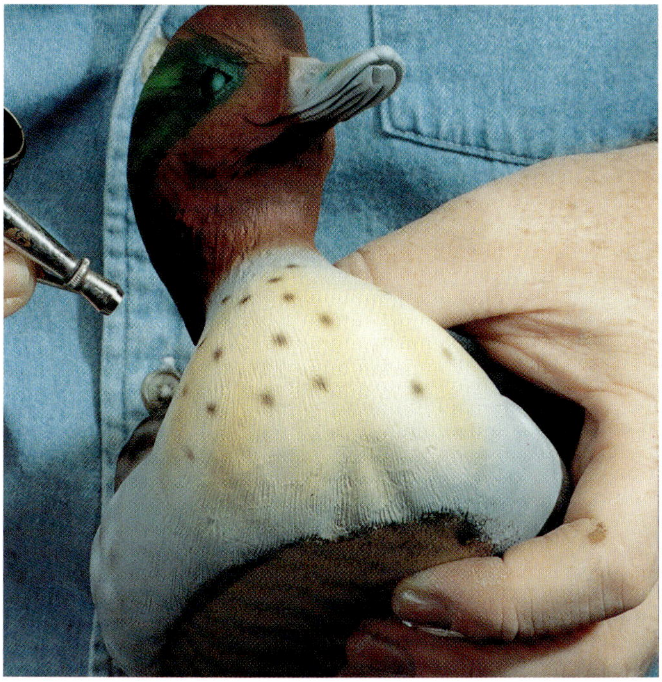

Now use the burnt umber to make some random dots on the chest. Most dots will need to be hit at least twice to get the proper intensity of color.

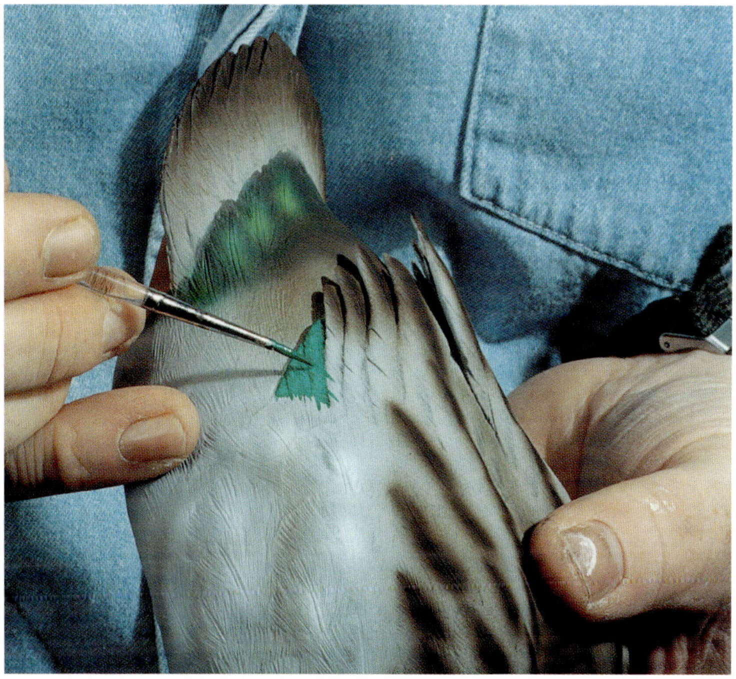

With a brush, apply a little iridescent green to the secondary patch of feathers on both sides.

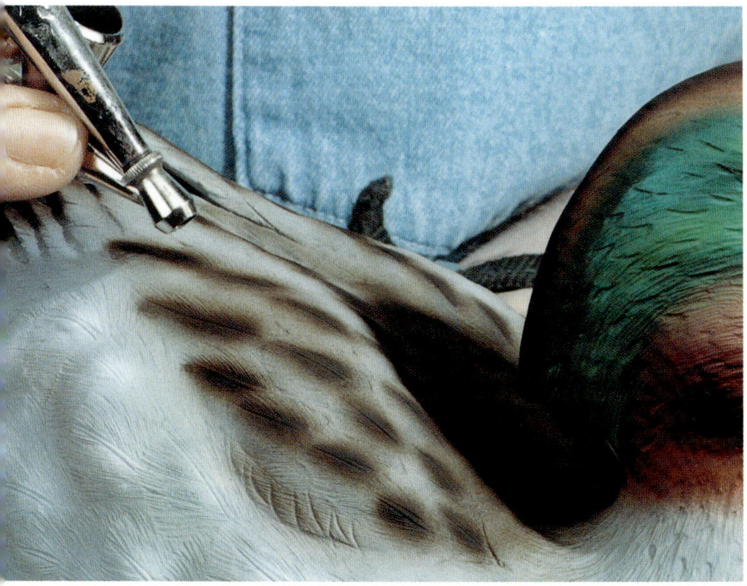

Shoot the center of each back feather with the burnt umber.

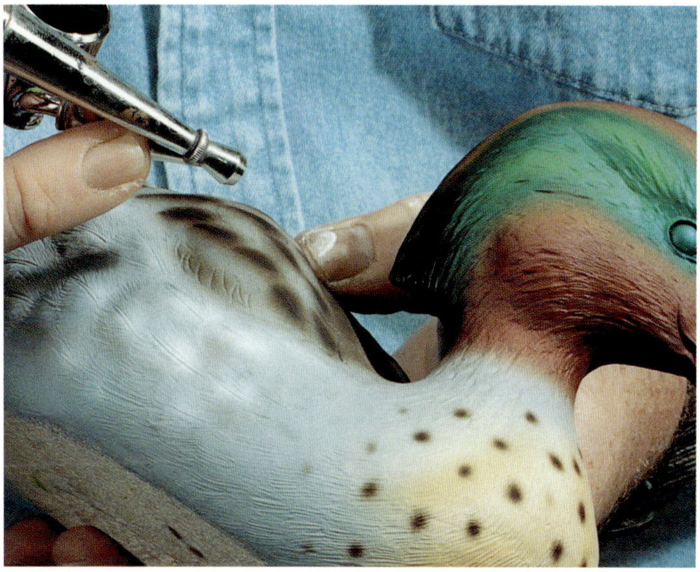

Spray black on the tip of the drake's crest.

Black is also sprayed on the lower edge of the scapular feathers.

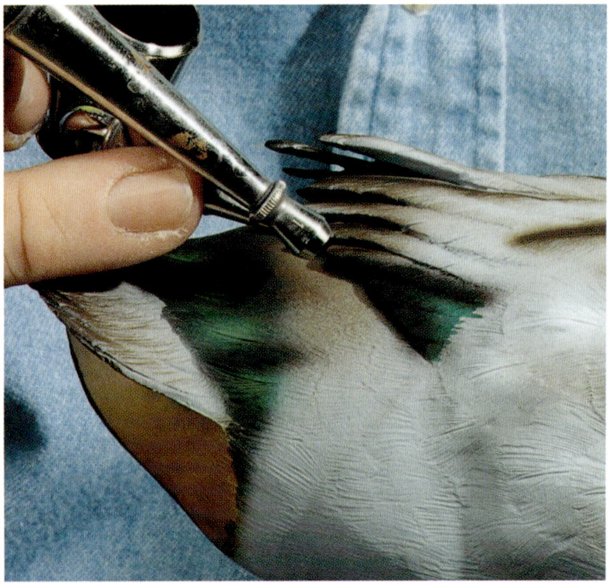

Apply black to the edges of the secondaries. I have also started applying black to the upper rump feathers (coverts).

Here's another view of the black that has been misted on the upper rump coverts.

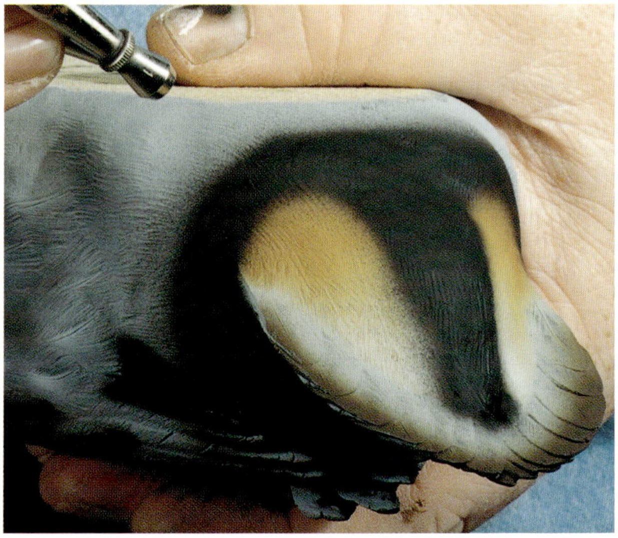

Finally, mist black around the yellow markings on the underrump. Follow the outline of the black applied earlier in the blocking stage.

Mix equal parts of white and yellow oxide and apply to the top edges of the upper rump coverts. All the airbrushing needed for now has been completed on the drake.

Airbrushing the Hen

The hen has far fewer colors than the drake. Start with straight white (remember, lighter colors first) and mist a little right where the bill meets the head, around the whole eye, and just behind the first cheek roll.

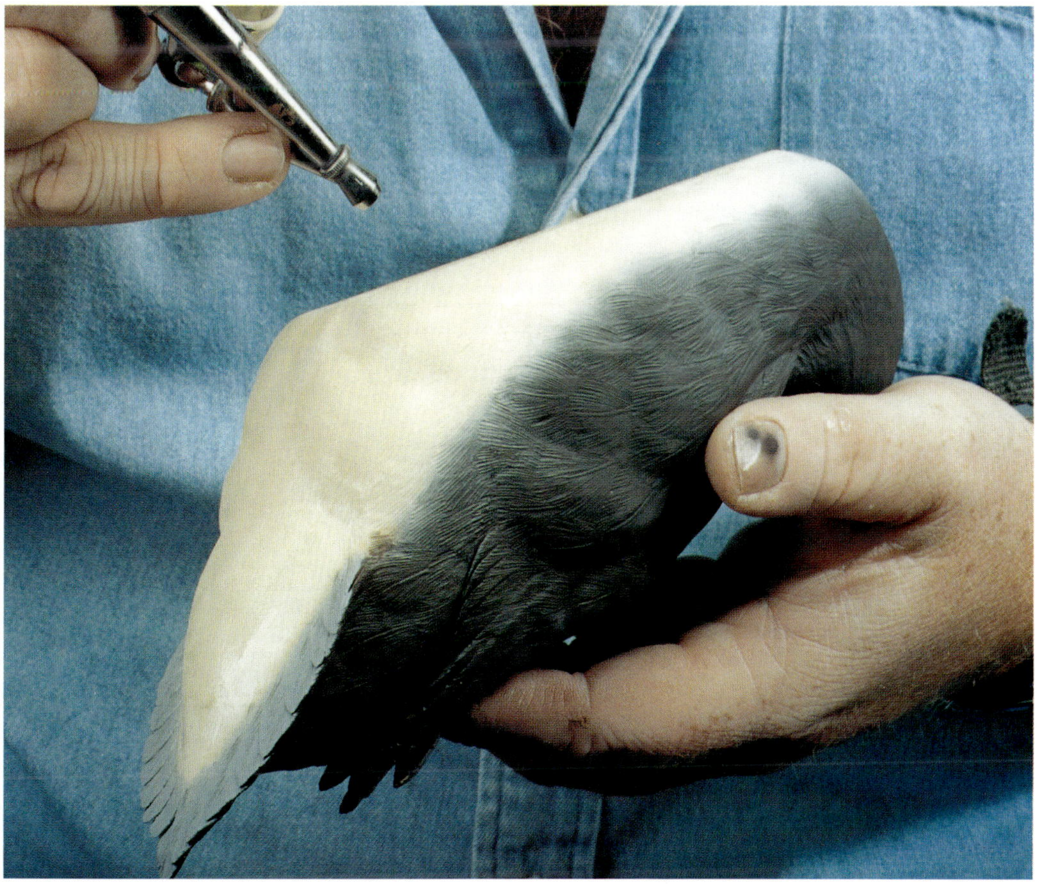

Mix approximately 60% white and 40% raw sienna to create a hen buff color. Spray this buff color where the two base coat colors meet to soften the transition between them.

Mist straight raw sienna along the crown line and back of the head. Mist just a little bit on the cheeks as well.

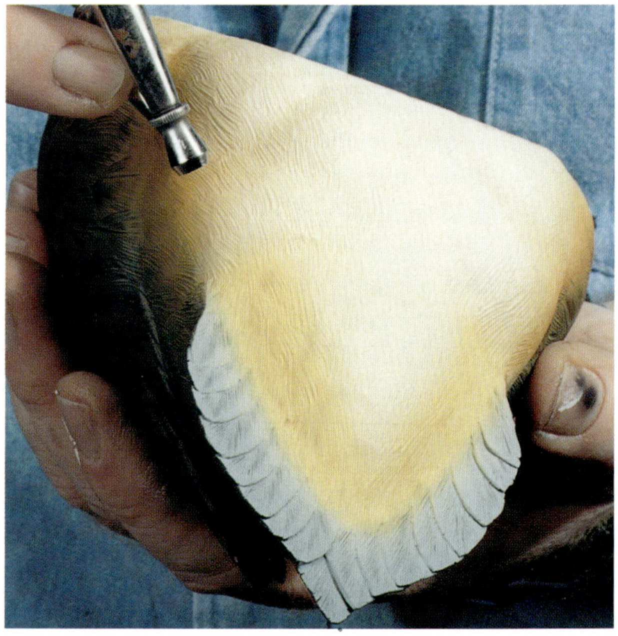

Mix equal parts of white and yellow oxide. Mist this mixture on the last row of underrump coverts.

Use straight raw sienna to blend in between the buff and brown base coats.

Mist hen brown (two thirds burnt umber and one third raw sienna) on the top of the head and back of the neck. Mist this right into the raw sienna to create a nice, soft blend of colors.

Now mist a little hen brown in front of and behind the eye to form a short eye line.

Mist a little more hen brown on the front and back of the cheek area. Note that any brown you see on the bill is only where I have practiced shooting the gun to be sure the paint is coming out properly.

Mist hen brown on the interior of all the underrump feathers.

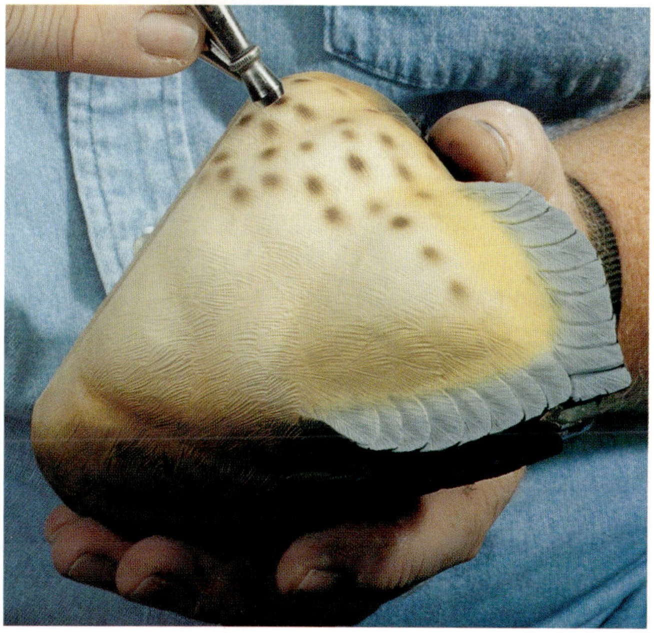

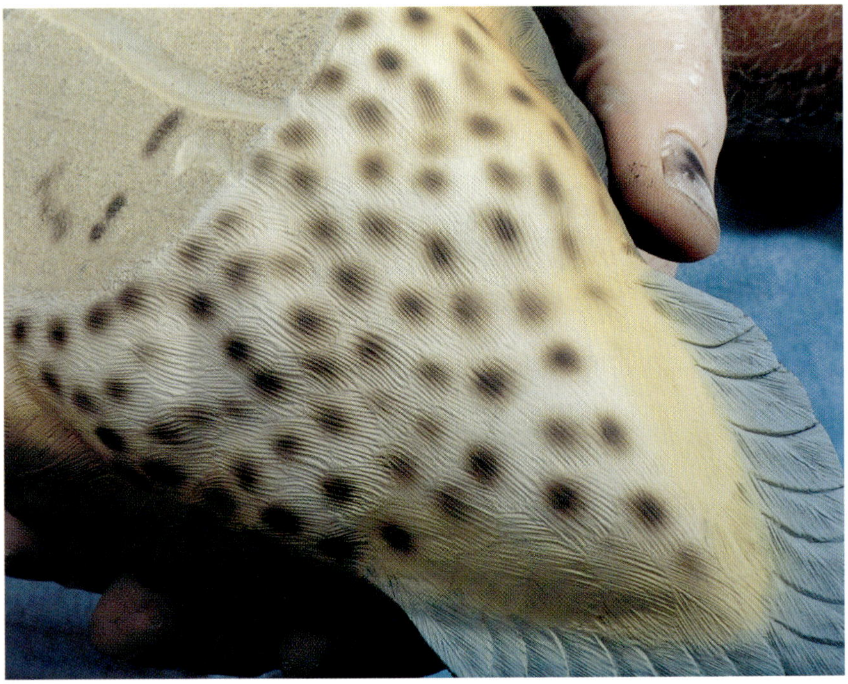

Here is the underrump with the previous step completed.

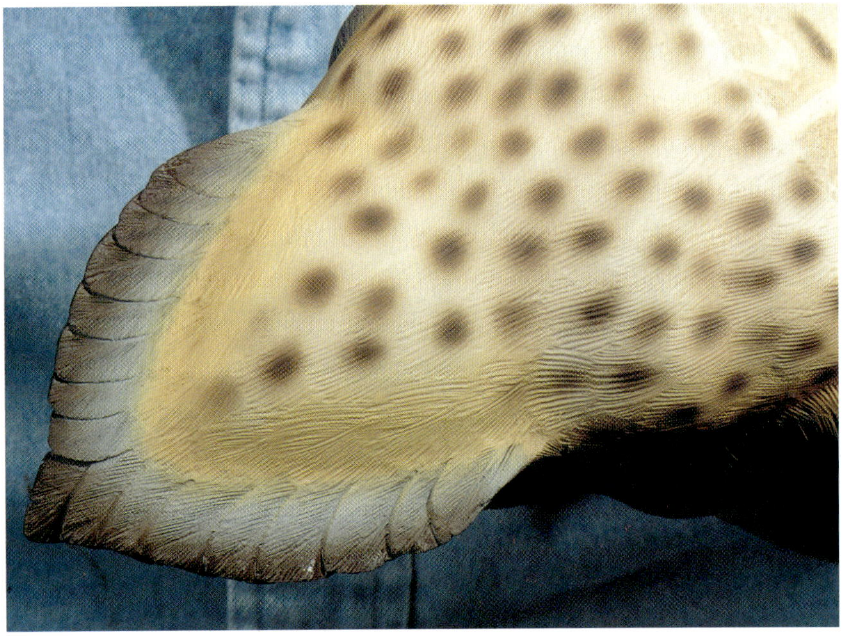

Haze some hen brown on the tips of the tail feathers, just like in the drake.

Mist hen brown along the side of the rump and ball area, blending it right into the raw sienna.

The back and top of the bird will be darker than the sides. Using straight burnt umber, spray the top of the wings and the top of the tail. It's a little hard to see in this picture, because the burnt umber is so similar to the brown gesso.

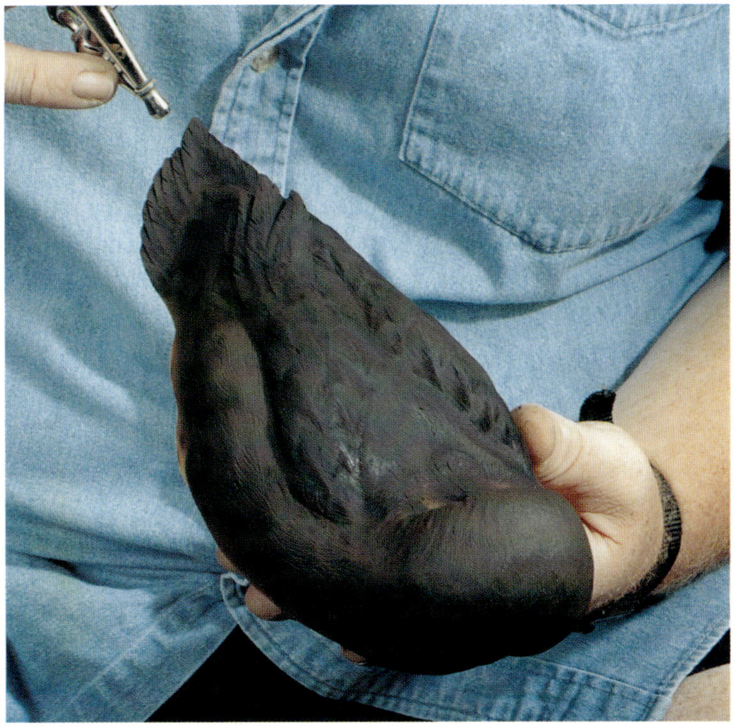

Mix approximately 70% white, 15% raw sienna, and 15% burnt umber to make a tan. Use this to lightly shoot the interior of the back and side feathers.

With a brush, paint the secondary patches iridescent green.

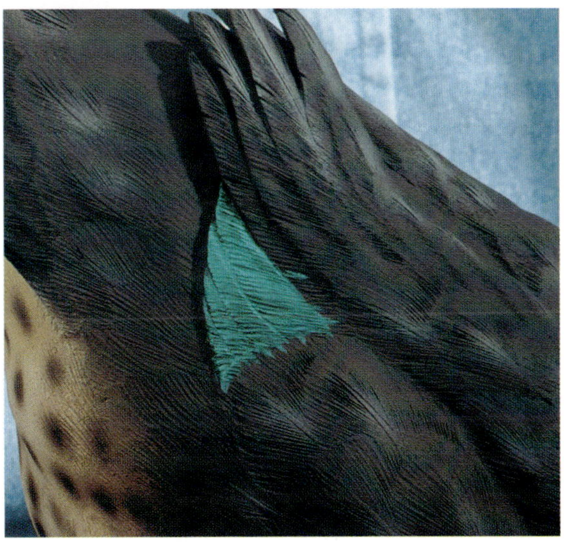

Still using the brush, apply straight gray on the exposed shoulder wing feathers.

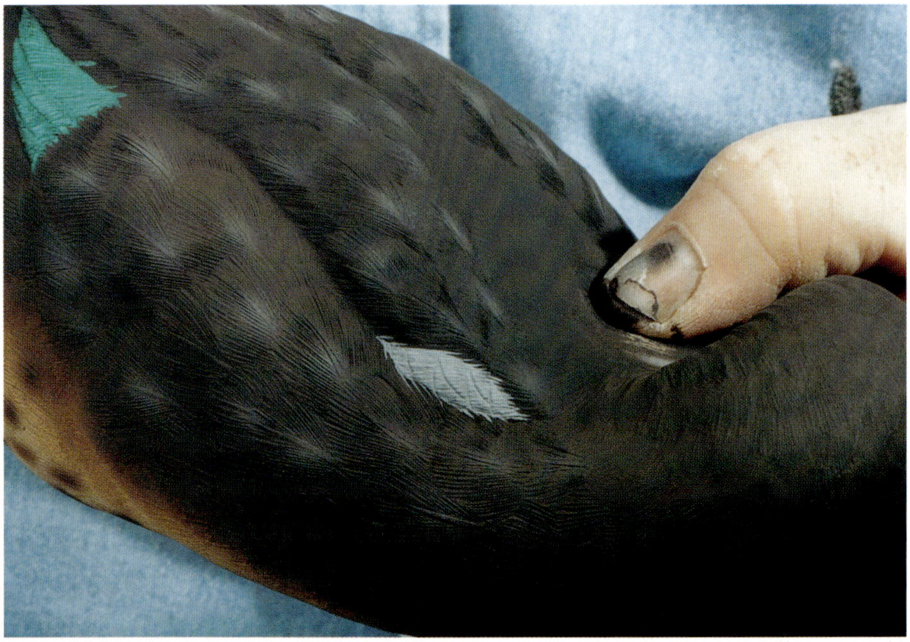

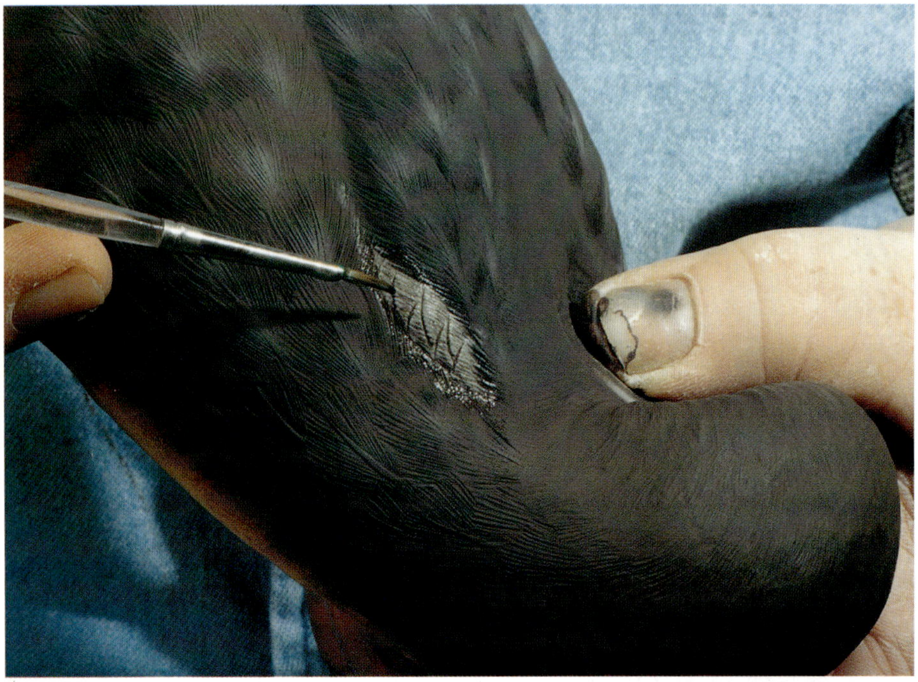

Then apply a wash of burnt umber over these feathers.

With the brush, paint the hen's bill straight gray.

Using the airbrush, apply a flesh or salmon color (70% white, 15% raw sienna, and 15% burnt sienna) to the whole lower edge of the bill.

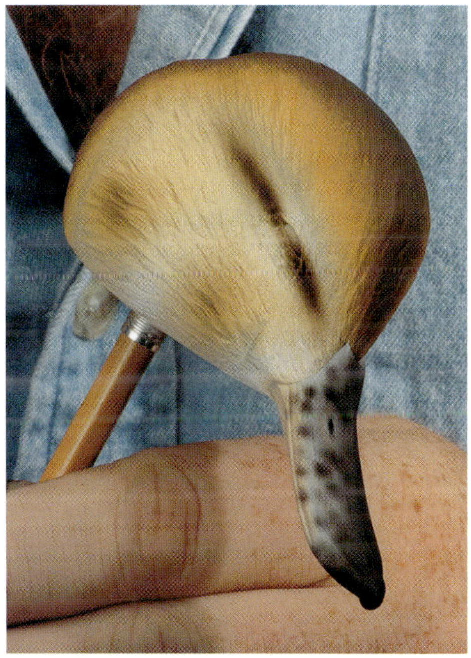

Use black to spray a series of dots on the upper mandible. Mist some black along the top of the mandible as well.

Mist some black through the middle and tip of the underside.

Just like on the drake, mist a little black along the edges of the secondaries.

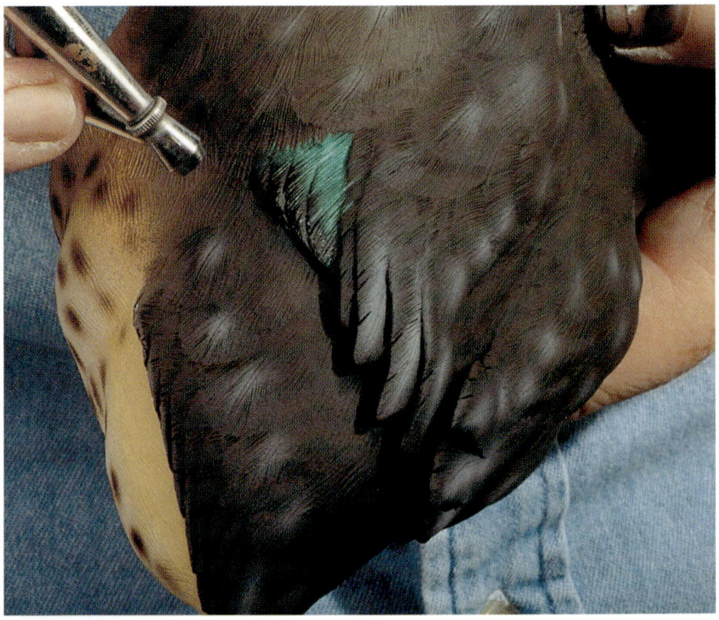

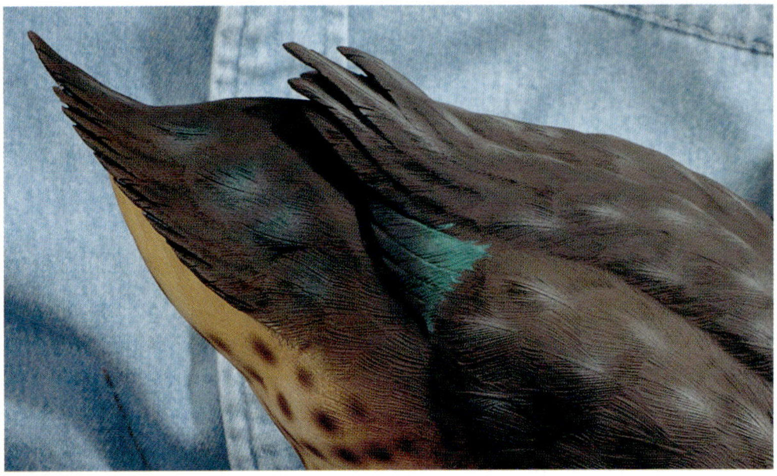

Spray a little iridescent green on the upper rump of the hen.

The hen to this point. Note that I have just set the head onto the body; it hasn't been attached yet.

Vermiculation, Edging, and Details on the Drake

We are ready to start the vermiculation on the drake. This will be done first on the side feathers, using a Yarka #5 red sable brush and very thin burnt umber paint. Fill the brush with paint, then drag the excess out. Dab the tip of the brush very lightly on each feather, creating a line of tiny dots. The lines of the vermiculation will go right through the quill. I strongly suggest you practice this step on a white piece of paper before trying it on the bird.

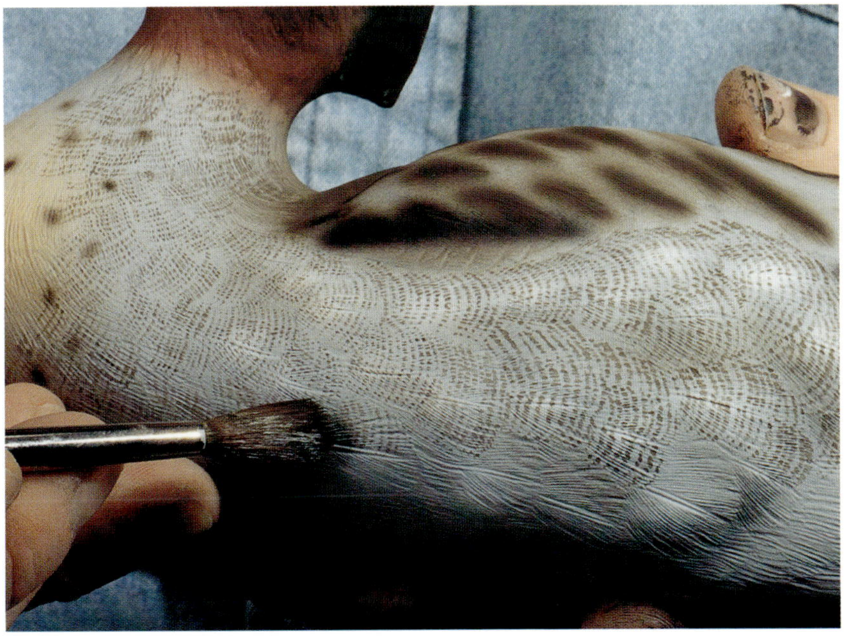

The vermiculation in progress along the side feathers.

When the vermiculation is completed, use the same brush to edge the feathers of the whole back and top of the tail with a mixture of 95% raw sienna and 5% white. Your paint should be of medium consistency. Fill the brush, drag the excess out, then "touch and pull" . . . touch the edge of the brush to the edge of the feather and pull back towards the interior.

Use the same technique on the tail. I have completed the left side only here to illustrate the difference.

The painted drake to this point.

Another view of the finished edging on the back and tail.

Go back over the same area and apply additional, very light edging to the back and tail feathers using white mixed with a tiny amount of raw sienna.

The white and raw sienna edging has been completed on the back . . .

. . . and the tail.

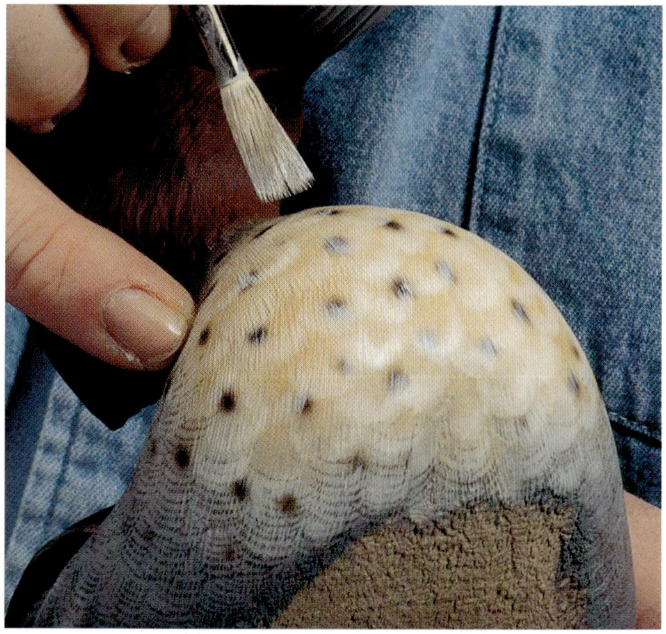

Using the same brush as before, edge the drake's chest with a mixture of 50% white and 50% raw sienna. Again, you should be aiming for a very subtle, light effect. Go right over the dots that were applied to the chest earlier, as needed. (More dots will be sprayed on the chest later in the process.)

With all the edging, it is important to use very thin paint and go over the areas more than once to achieve the correct color intensity. Here I am using straight white for the last pass over the chest edging.

The chest edging completed.

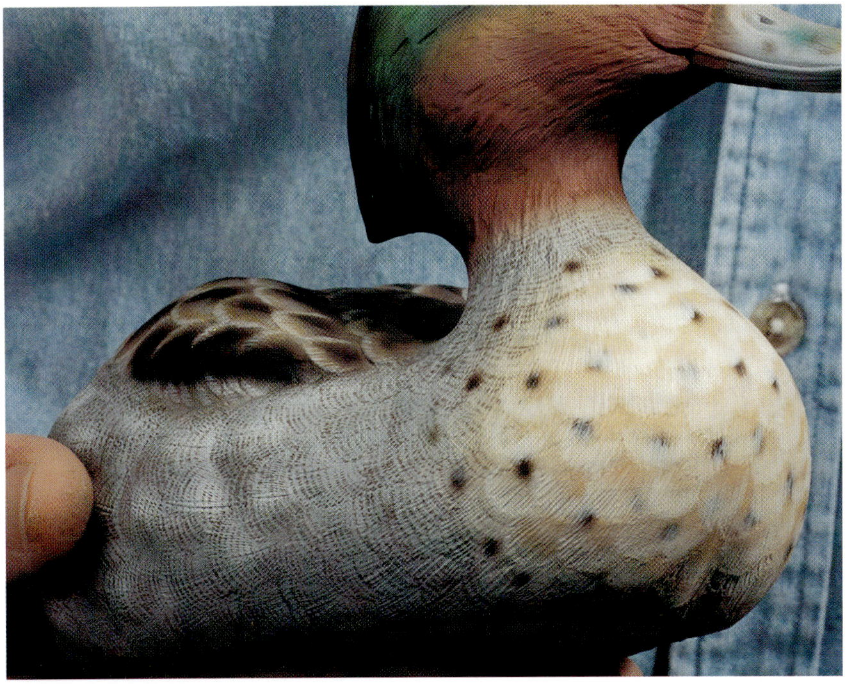

Edge the upper rump feathers with 50% white and 50% raw sienna.

Using a brush, vermiculate the back of the bird. The color (burnt umber) and technique are the same as that used for the side feathers. Apply vermiculation to all the scapular feathers of the back, but not to the last three tertials.

Continuing the vermiculation on the back. Remember to keep your paint thin and always drag the excess from your brush. Better to go back over an area a second time if needed than to apply the paint too heavily the first time.

The completed vermiculation on the back.

Use the same color (burnt umber) to vermiculate the upper rump feathers.

Using your brush, apply a fine line of 50% black and 50% burnt umber down the center of each feather to darken and define the quills.

To define the splits, apply an even finer line with the same color along the depressions carved earlier with the ruby.

Complete the painting of the quills and splits on the entire back, rump, and tail area of the bird. Your drake should look like this when you are done.

Use white to define the splits on the side feathers. The process is the same as for the back and tail, just a different color.

Apply fine white lines for the quills on the underside of the tail feathers.

Edge the feathers on the lower part of the ball area and rump with white.

I have completed the white splits on the side feathers and the white edging along the bottom.

Apply a burnt umber wash on the back, sides, and top of the tail, to tie everything together. Your wash should be about 20% paint and 80% water. You may need to apply more than one wash; again, it's better to start with a very light coat and add more if necessary. Make sure the bird is thoroughly dry in between the washes.

I've put two washes on my drake to achieve just the degree of softness I'm looking for.

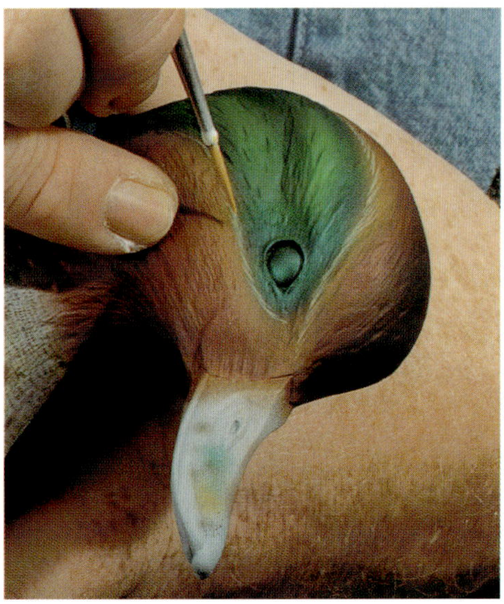

Using a No. 2 round brush, paint the fringes around the green patch on the head with a combination of 50% white and 50% yellow oxide. Use very delicate, fine strokes, coming back over them as necessary with your brush. Note that the upper fringe extends to the tip of the bill.

The fringe should look like this when you are done.

Now add a little more white to your paint and go back over the fringe with this lighter color. The subtle difference may be hard to see in the picture but it adds some highlights to the fringe.

Use the 50/50 yellow oxide and white color to define the outer edges of the upper rump feathers. I'm still using the No. 2 round brush.

As with the fringe around the green patch, come back over the same feathers with a much lighter shade of yellow oxide and white. You should be able to see the additional depth and realism this step provides.

Use the 50/50 yellow oxide and white color to edge the yellow markings on the underrump.

Then come back with the lighter shade (almost white, with just a little yellow oxide mixed in), the same as on the head fringe and the upper rump feathers.

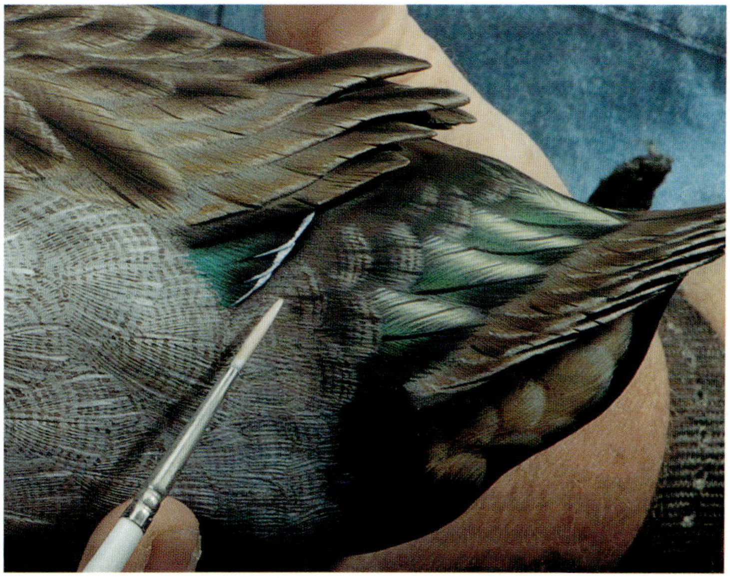

Use straight white to very lightly and finely paint the stripe on the edge of the secondaries.

Paint the entire bill black. Be very careful around the area where the bill meets the head, so you don't damage any of the previous work done on the head. You will probably need two coats for the bill.

Paint the quills and splits of the upper rump feathers black. This really sets off the tail feathers nicely as well.

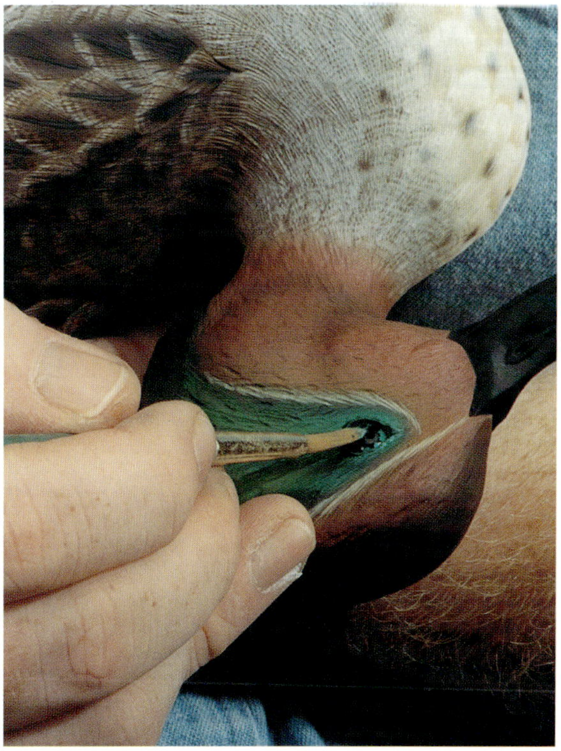

Use a damp brush to clean off any paint from the eyes.

Once the eyes are cleaned, paint the eyelids with burnt umber. This addition is very subtle, but helps to make the eyelid area a bit darker than the green around it.

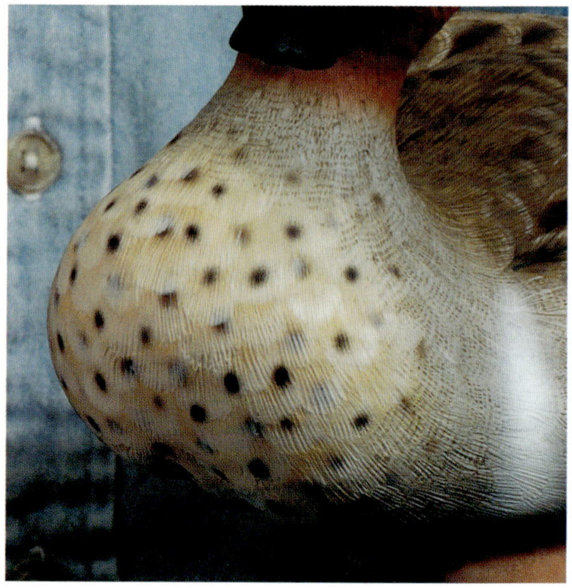

Now spray additional dots on the chest with black. Using burnt umber for the earlier dots gives this area a layered effect, creating the illusion of depth.

Thin down some white and black to use with the airbrush. First apply the drake's characteristic white markings right in front of the shoulder on the ball area.

To add greater realism to the quills, go over them with a clear gloss. They should end up looking shiny, like fingernails. Coat the bill with a mixture of 50% gloss and 50% matte, giving it more of a leathery appearance. Other than adding the primaries, our drake is finished.

Edging and Details on the Hen

The hen will be edged using three different colors. Start with 80% raw sienna and 20% white and use this to edge the sides, back, chest, and tail. I've done a good bit here already.

The first color edging completed.

To soften this first edging, come back with burnt umber in the gun and shoot towards the interior of each feather.

The hen to this point.

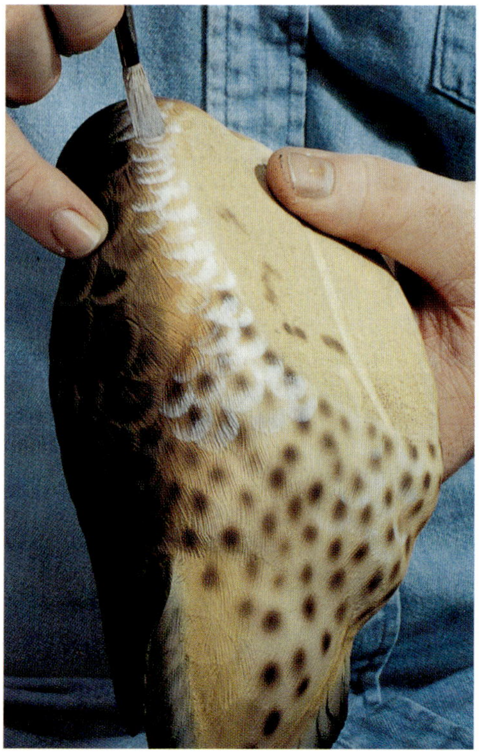

Edge the underrump area and below the ball area on the sides with straight white.

Edge the sides, back, chest, and tail a second time with 80% white and 20% raw sienna. Apply this just to the tip of the feather and don't pull back as far as the previous edging, allowing the first color to show through. I've completed most of this on the left hand side here.

All the edging has now been completed. Here is a top view . .

. . . and an underside view.

Using your brush and straight raw sienna, begin the interior markings of the feathers. The top feathers will have far fewer markings than those on the side.

The previous step completed.

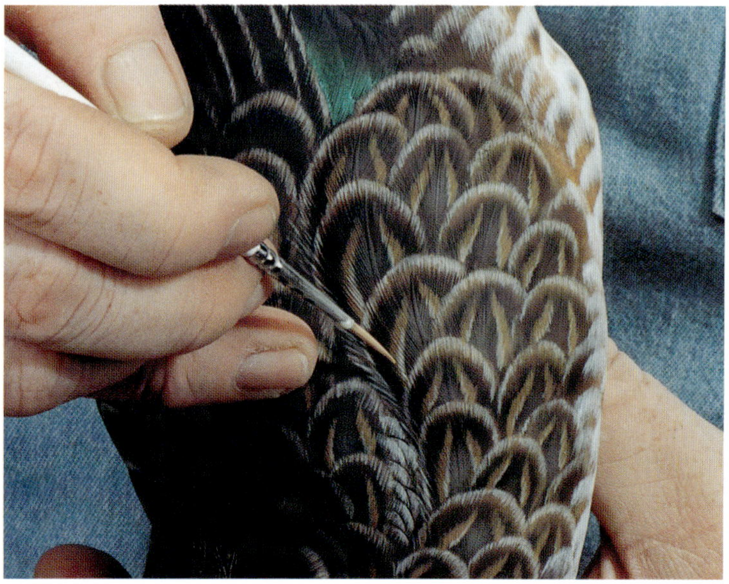

Add some highlights to the interior markings using white mixed with a little raw sienna. Apply just a tiny amount of this color to the inside edge of the interior markings. Do this on all the feathers of the side and back.

As with the drake, we will use a combination of 50% black and 50% burnt umber for the quills and splits. To define the quills, draw a fine line with this color down the center of each feather on the top, the sides, and the top of the tail.

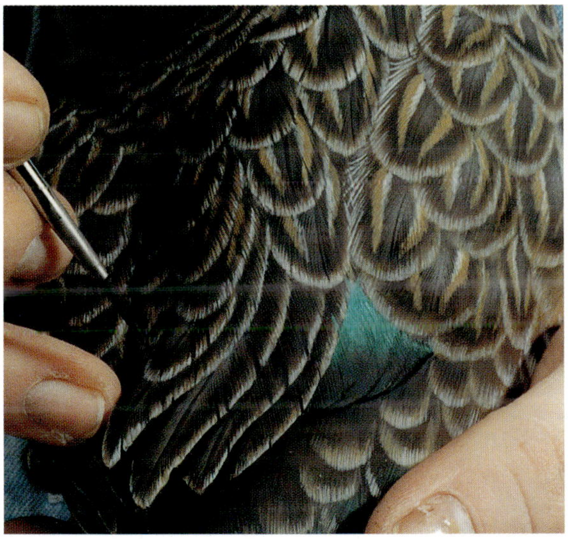

The technique for the splits is the same as that used for the drake: apply an even finer line along the depressions carved earlier with the ruby. I come right into the interior markings of the feather to break them up as well.

The quills and splits completed.

Apply a wash of 50% burnt umber and 50% raw sienna over the top, sides, top of the tail, and chest (all the brown areas). I recommend using two thin coats for this wash.

Define the quills on the underside of the tail with straight white.

As on the drake, use straight white to very lightly and finely paint the stripes of the secondaries.

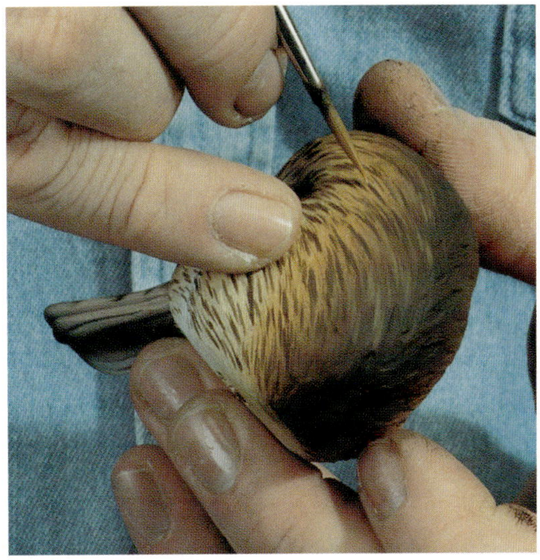

Starting at the back of the head, flick raw sienna right into the rest of the head. Go over some of the brown marks and next to others.

We will use three different colors for the "flicks" on the hen's head (the little interior markings of the head feathers). Start the flicks with 50% raw sienna and 50% burnt umber.

The second of the three colors completed.

The first of the three colors completed.

Mix 50% white and 50% raw sienna for the last of the three flick colors. Here is the head with all three colors completed.

Add some extra flicking with straight white just underneath the hen's partially closed eye.

Clean any excess paint off the eyes using a brush and apply a little burnt umber on the eyelid. The technique for both these steps is the same as that used on the drake.

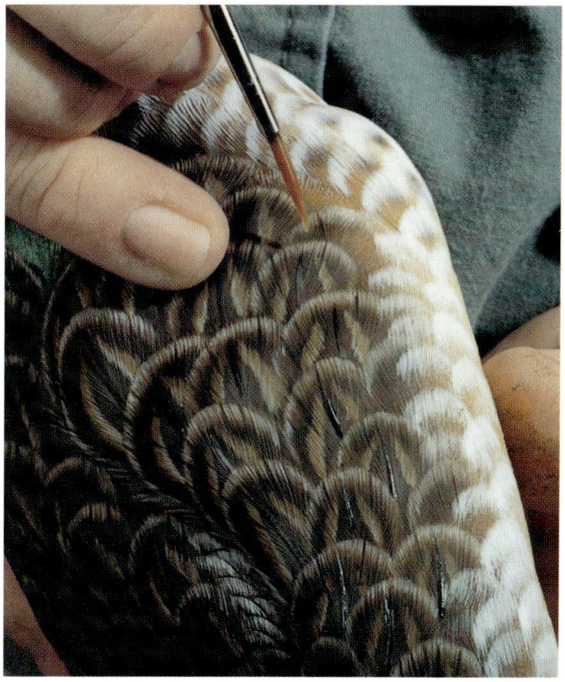

Gloss the quills, then gloss and matte the bill. I use straight gloss thinned with a little water to go over the quills and 50% gloss mixed with 50% matte for the bill. Quills are first . . .

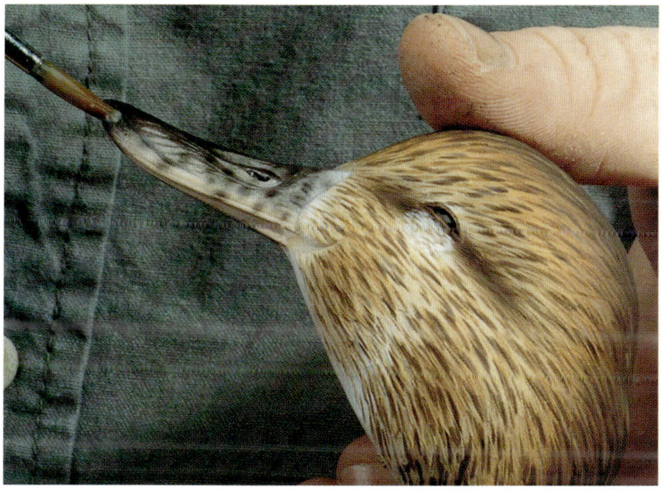

. . . then the bill.

The quills and bill completed. To attach the hen's head, use equal amounts of two part five minute epoxy. Place a small amount in the hole at the base of the head and a small amount in the chest pocket. Set the head in place and allow to dry. Other than the primaries, the hen is finished.

Primaries

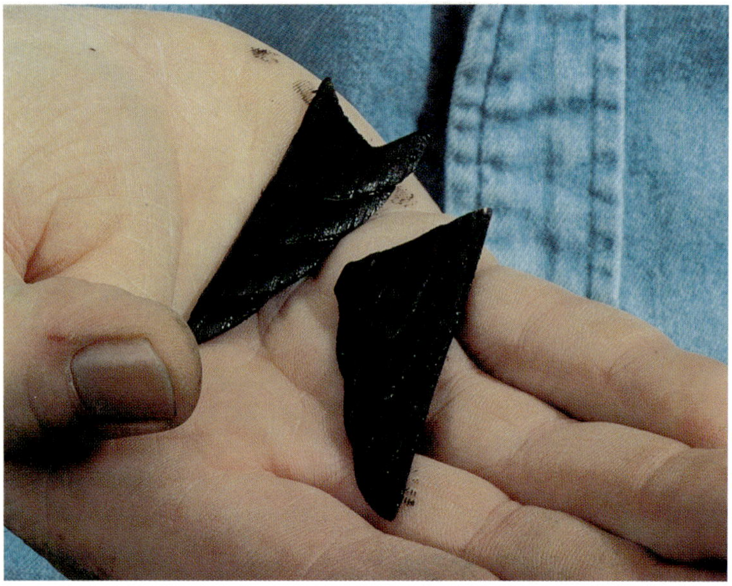

Painting of the primaries is the same for the drake and hen. Start by applying two coats of burnt umber with your brush.

Mix approximately 70% white, 15% raw sienna, and 15% burnt umber to obtain tan. Spray this on the interior of the top side.

Using the airbrush, mist gray on the interior of the underside.

Lightly edge each of the primary feathers with the same tan used in the previous step.

Paint the white quill on the underside of each primary.

Here are the two primaries with the quills and splits completed.

Paint the dark quills and splits on the top of the primaries using 50% burnt umber and 50% black.

Apply a burnt umber wash to both of the primaries. As before, two thin coats are recommended. Then gloss the quills, using straight gloss thinned with a little water. Both steps have been completed here.

To attach the primaries, mix equal parts of five minute epoxy. Apply a small amount to the top and bottom of the wider end and slip the primary into its spot on the back of the bird.

The same view showing correct placement of the first primary . . .

For assistance with placement, here is the back end of the hen before the primaries are attached.

. . . and the second primary.

The completed drake.

The completed hen.

Gallery

Green-Wing Teal Drake